# GLOBETROTTER

*Th*

# MALTA

## BRIAN RICHARDS

NEW
HOLLAND

# GLOBETROTTER™

First edition published in 2002
by New Holland Publishers (UK) Ltd
London • Cape Town • Sydney • Auckland
10 9 8 7 6 5 4 3 2 1

website: www.newhollandpublishers.com

Garfield House, 86 Edgware Road
London W2 2EA
United Kingdom

80 McKenzie Street
Cape Town 8001
South Africa

14 Aquatic Drive
Frenchs Forest, NSW 2086
Australia

218 Lake Road
Northcote, Auckland
New Zealand

Distributed in the USA by
The Globe Pequot Press, Connecticut

ISBN 1 84330 292 6

**Publishing Manager (UK):** Simon Pooley
**Publishing Manager (SA):** John Loubser
**Managing Editor:** Thea Grobbelaar
**DTP Cartographic Manager:** Genené Hart
**Editor:** Melany McCallum
**Designer:** Lellyn Creamer
**Cover Design:** Lellyn Creamer, Nicole Engeler
**Cartographer:** Nicole Engeler
**Proofreader:** Vanessa Rogers

Reproduction by Resolution (Cape Town) and
Hirt & Carter (Pty) Ltd, Cape Town
Printed and bound in Hong Kong by Sing Cheong
Printing Co. Ltd.

**Dedication:**
To my wife Sandra, as enthusiastic a visitor to
Malta over the past 20 years as myself, and
daughter Claire.

**Acknowledgements:**
The publishers and author gratefully acknowledge
the generous assistance during the compilation of
this book of Air Malta; Belleair Holidays; Corinthia
Group of Companies; Malta Tourist Office,
London; Malta Tourism Authority; Suncrest
Hotel, Qawra.

**Photographic Credits:**
**AA Photo Library**, page 62
**Brian Richards**, front cover, title page, pages
6, 10, 13, 14, 15, 18, 20, 23, 25, 26, 27, 30,
31, 33, 34, 36, 37, 38, 40, 41, 43, 47, 50, 53,
54, 60, 61, 63, 64, 70, 71, 74, 75, 76, 78, 79,
81, 82
**Mary Evans Picture Library**, pages 9, 72
**Paul Murphy**, pages 7, 8, 22, 32, 44, 84
**Robert Harding Picture Library**, pages 11, 12,
16, 19, 21, 28, 29, 35, 39, 45, 46, 48, 49, 52,
65, 80, 83
**Sylvia Cordaiy Photo Library/Johnathan
Smith**, page 73
**Travel Ink/Rawdon Wyatt**, page 17

**Front Cover:** Old harbour walls and fishing
boats crowd in alongside modern holiday apartments along the north coast of Malta at St
Paul's Bay.

**Title Page:** Brightly painted luzzu fishing boats
tied up in Marsaxlokk harbour.

# CONTENTS

## MAKE THE MOST OF YOUR GUIDE

Reading these two pages will help you to get the most out of your guide and save you time when using it. Sites discussed in the text are cross-referenced with the cover maps – for example, the reference 'Map B–C3' refers to the Gozo Map (Map B), column C, row 3. Use the Map Plan below to quickly locate the map you need.

### MAP PLAN

Outside Back Cover                                    Outside Front Cover

Inside Front Cover                                    Inside Back Cover

### THE BIGGER PICTURE

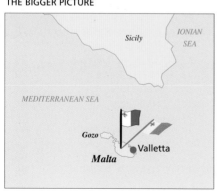

**Key to Map Plan**
A – Victoria
B – Gozo
C – St Paul's Bay and Buġibba
D – Malta
E – Mdina
F – Rabat
G – Sliema and St Julian's
H – Valletta
I  – The Three Cities
J – Bus Routes
K – Excursions

## Key to Symbols

⊠ — address

☎ — telephone

☏ — fax

🖳 — website

☝ — e-mail address

🕓 — opening times

🚃 — tour

⏱ — entry fee

🍽 — restaurants nearby

## Map Legend

| | | | |
|---|---|---|---|
| national road | main road | Museum |
| main road | other road | St Paul |
| minor road | built-up area | |
| river | *Wied ir-Rum* | post office | ⊠ |
| city | VALLETTA | wall | |
| | | ferry | |
| major town | ⊙ Rabat | parking | P |
| town | ○ St Julian's | police station | ● |
| large village | ◎ Marsascala | hospital | ⊕ |
| village | ○ Fontana | bus terminus | |
| peak in metres | Il Pellegrin ▲ 127 m | library | |
| cave | Blue Grotto | place of interest | • Tarxien Temples |
| ruin | | hotel | Ⓗ OSBORNE |
| viewpoint | | place of worship | △ Church of Gesu |
| water sports | Ⓦ | tourist information | ⓘ |
| swimming | | airport | ⊕ ⊕ |
| diving | | golf course | |
| beach | | park & garden | Gardjola Garden |

## Keep us Current

Travel information is apt to change, which is why we regularly update our guides. We'd be most grateful to receive feedback from you if you've noted something we should include in our updates. If you have any new information, please share it with us by writing to the Publishing Manager, Globetrotter, at the office nearest to you (addresses on the imprint page of this guide). The most significant contribution to each new edition will be rewarded with a free copy of the updated guide.

**Above:** *A poppy field colours the countryside above Salina Bay.*

## OVERVIEW

Rugged limestone outcrops rising out of the glittering Mediterranean Sea, the Maltese islands are a fascinating blend of history, holidays and friendly small-island hospitality.

## The Land

Malta is both the name of the nation and of the largest of the Maltese islands; Gozo is about 8km (5 miles) to the northwest of Malta, and midway between them is Comino. The island group, which also includes uninhabited Filfla and Cominotto, extends for 45km (28 miles) from northwest to southeast in the centre of the Mediterranean basin.

The islands offer contrasting scenery. Malta largely comprises a limestone plateau, Gozo is blessed with an underlying layer of blue clay and tiny Comino is barren in the extreme.

The sea is clean and clear, pleasant to bathe in, excellent for diving and accommodates a wide array of water sports. Some of Malta's best beaches are in the far north, where stretches of golden sand fill the bays either side of Marfa Ridge. Steep cliffs characterize Malta's southern shore.

### Flora and Fauna

**Wildlife** is scarce and restricted to reptiles and birds. The reservoirs of Chadwick Lakes near Rabat and the Għadira Nature Reserve at Mellieħa Bay are the only bird habitats in Malta, providing sightings in spring and early autumn.

**Wild flowers** abound in autumn, winter and spring – more than 600 varieties carpet the islands with a blaze of colour.

## History in Brief

Long before man arrived, the Maltese islands were joined to Europe and Africa. The first people arrived about 7000 years ago from Sicily, which is only 93km (58 miles) away. These were early **Neolithic** people who farmed and reared animals, used stone implements, made pottery and eked out an existence in isolated communities.

Later generations were the builders of ancient temples and tombs cut from rock; awe-inspiring handiwork dating from before 2000BC which can still be seen throughout Malta and Gozo. Successive incursions of Bronze Age colonists followed before the arrival of **Phoenician** civilization in Malta around the 9th century BC.

The Phoenicians traded with the western Mediterranean and initially sought refuge in Malta's natural harbours. They brought prosperity to the islands, which subsequently came under the influence of their descendants, the **Carthaginians** – who, from their base in Tunis, gave Malta strategic importance for the first time. With Rome's influence in southern Italy growing, conflict between the **Romans** and Carthaginians was inevitable. In the firing line, Malta became a military base in the **First Punic War** (262–242BC), when it was sacked by the Romans. Although the Carthaginians regained control, Malta was seized again by the Romans in the **Second Punic War** (218BC) and stayed tied to Rome.

Malta prospered under Roman rule and important towns developed. However, Malta retained

**Barbarity in War**
The fall of Fort St Elmo to the Turks on 23 June 1565 precipitated savagery unmatched at any stage in the battle. The Turkish commander ordered the decapitation of several Knights; the heads were impaled on stakes and the torsos, nailed to planks, were set adrift in Grand Harbour. Four bodies reached the opposite shore, prompting immediate retaliation from Grand Master La Valette. He ordered the execution of all the Turkish prisoners in Fort St Angelo, loaded the heads into cannons and fired them back across Grand Harbour at the Turks in Fort St Elmo.

**Below:** *Philippe Villiers de l'Isle Adam, first Grand Master on Malta.*

**Opposite:** *An Italian publication records the wartime air raids on Malta.*
**Below:** *Symbol of an island republic: the familiar Maltese Cross was introduced by the knights in the mid-16th century.*

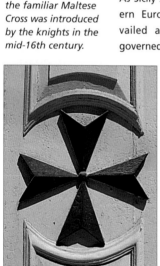

many Phoenician influences and opinion is still divided over whether Malta's name origi-nates in the Phoenician *malat*, meaning port, or the Roman *meli*, meaning honey. It was under the Romans that one of the most important happenings in Maltese history occurred – the shipwreck of St Paul the Apostle on Malta in AD60 and the conversion of the islands to Christianity.

With the decline of the Roman Empire in the fifth century, Malta found new masters in the **Byzantines**. In AD870, the **Arabs** con-quered Malta from their base in Sicily and held the island for more than two centuries. Their influence still shows in the Maltese language spoken today and the many place names of Arab origin.

When Count Roger the **Norman** led an invasion from his kingdom in Sicily in 1090 and restored Christianity under Norman rule, the Arabs were allowed to remain for a while. As Sicily switched hands, so did Malta; west-ern European influences increasingly pre-vailed and by 1282, Malta found itself governed by the **Spanish**.

In 1530, Holy Roman Emperor Charles V granted Malta to the **Knights of the Order of St John of Jerusalem**; their stay as masters of Malta lasted until the 1798 capitu-lation to Napoleon's **French** forces.

Maltese life under the French was brief. In 1800, the **British** assumed control and the 1814 Treaty of Paris confirmed Malta's status under the British crown for 150 years, until the granting of independence in 1964. The Maltese islands, once more of

high strategic importance, played a heroic role during World War II in the face of incredible odds which earned them the George Cross. In 1974, Malta became a republic within the Commonwealth.

## Government and Economy

When independent Malta became a republic on 13 December 1974, economic stability was the priority facing Prime Minister **Dom Mintoff**. Ties with Britain were severed in March 1979, leaving Malta to seek economic assistance elsewhere.

The British military withdrawal, at the end of an extended defence agreement made at independence in 1964, had a drastic effect on employment. Job losses were partly offset by widespread **emigration** to Canada and Australia; today as many Maltese live abroad as in the islands themselves.

In the mid-1970s, Mintoff declared a policy of neutrality, cultivating closer friendships outside Europe with the likes of Russia, China and Libya which gave rise to unease in Europe. But the fears born out of Mintoff's worldly fraternizations proved without foundation – the previous Nationalist government had pledged its future to Europe through an EEC association agreement, forerunner to Malta's initial application for full **European Union** membership in 1990.

Participation in Malta's two-party politics is a national pastime. Clubs for **Nationalist** and **Labour** followers proliferate, an indication of

### The Santa Maria Convoy

In the summer of 1942, Malta was in dire need of food and fuel to continue its struggle against the Axis powers. As the Maltese prayed to Santa Maria, whose feast day was due on 15 August, Britain sent a convoy of 14 merchant ships under armed escort. As the ships neared Malta, they came under massive air and sea attack. Nine merchant ships were sunk; the five remaining included the tanker *Ohio*, with 11,000 tons of fuel critical to Malta's survival. On 13 August four vessels limped into Grand Harbour. More prayers were offered to Santa Maria and on the morning of the 15th, the *Ohio* reached Malta. The islands were saved and the name of the Santa Maria Convoy became legendary.

**Above:** *Soon after it was awarded to Malta in 1942, the George Cross became an important icon on Malta's National Flag.*

the close inter-party rivalry. After three consecutive spells in government, the Labour party found itself shunted out in 1987 by the Nationalists. **Dr Carmelo Mifsud Bonnici**, having replaced Mintoff as Prime Minister in 1984, was forced out of office three years later. **Dr Eddie Fenech-Adami** took over the House of Representatives. Under the Nationalists, who were re-elected in 1992, and again in 1998 after a brief Labour period, Malta has taken a firm pro-Europe stance, feeling that full EU membership will strengthen its policy of non-alignment.

While other Mediterranean holiday destinations have seen their fortunes ebb and flow, Malta's popularity appears to know no bounds. Each year sees an increase in tourist numbers, with an all-time high of more than 1.2 million in 2001. Tourism is now Malta's principal industry, providing 24% of the country's gross national product. The highly impressive **Malta International Airport** terminal, able to handle 2.5 million departing passengers a year, was opened in 1992; two years later the new **cruise ship terminal** below Valletta's bastions received the first of many white-hulled cruise liners.

Shipping continues to play a significant role in the economy, with Malta's dockyards successfully tendering for servicing and repair work on tankers and container ships plying the Mediterranean. Additionally, the Malta **Freeport** distribution centre is well established as a foreign exchange earner. **Agriculture** also makes a solid contribution, despite the compact nature of Malta and Gozo.

## The People

To the visitor, the locals might all be Maltese, but those from Gozo will claim they are Gozitan first, Maltese second. There has always been friendly rivalry between the two, with Malta people telling jokes about the 'mean' Gozitans and Gozo folk forever claiming intellectual superiority.

Down the centuries, despite domination by a succession of expansionist-minded invaders, the Maltese have clung to their strong insular identity. Gregarious by nature among themselves, they are generally friendly towards visitors, though it may be noticed that those in the service industry often make little effort to please.

Typically among Latin races, the Maltese are devoted to the **family** and family life. Families are often large and stay closely in touch; in such a small island community parents, brothers, sisters, aunts, uncles and their various offspring all live within a short distance of each other.

As business in Malta tends to be male dominated, women are left to play the traditional home-caring role. It is today's generation of daughters, keen to develop their own careers, who are freeing themselves from the constraints of the past.

Attitudes to **dress** are conventional in Malta, a country of firm social traditions. Visitors should be suitably attired when entering churches to save causing offence. Topless sunbathing is against the law.

> **Close Families**
> It is said that a dozen Maltese family names are shared by 90% of the population; after a short time in Malta you will be familiar with most of them. Among the most popular surnames are Azzopardi, Borg, Calleja, Camilleri, Caruana, Galea, Gatt, Grech, Pace, Tabona, Vella and Zammit. Maltese families remain close-knit, continuing to live in the same town or village or often the same street. Don't be surprised to see a family gathering of 30 or more enjoying Sunday lunch together in a restaurant.

**Below:** *There's always time for a chat; men catch up on the local gossip in Republic Street, Valletta.*

# OVERVIEW

## Sacred Spots

Malta's religious character shows in the number of shrines dotted about the islands – by the wayside and on street corners; even set in the wall of Valletta's ruined Opera House. Flickering candles in their red see-through holders and fresh flowers are an ever-present reminder of the Maltese people's strong religious convictions. Builders of Malta's old buses often incorporated a small shrine behind the driver; some bone-shaking vehicles prominently spread the word that 'Jesus Lives'.

## Language

Such is the Maltese familiarity with English that visitors need concern themselves only with the pronunciation of place names. Determined linguists will discover that the Maltese language of Malti, Phoenician-based with Arab modifications and later English and Italian influences, is complex and not the easiest to speak or understand.

## Religion

Malta's Roman Catholic roots run deep. The majority of the population is devoutly Catholic and the Church plays a large part in their lives, as is shown by the size of the churches in even the smallest villages. The islands have more than 350 churches, from the awesome edifices of St John's Co-Cathedral (see page 14) in Valletta and Xewkija's parish church on Gozo, down to those the size of the tiny chapel on Comino.

With four out of five Maltese regularly attending mass, the need for so many churches is readily apparent. Not all are in permanent use, however – some isolated chapels are unlocked only on feast days. Nearly all services are held in Malti.

**Below:** *Maltese woman in national dress, with one of the islands' lively* luzzu *fishing boats.*

Throughout the islands, **Holy Week** has special meaning. Large crowds turn out in towns and villages for the Good Friday processions. Local organizations march slowly at the head of the procession, focal point of which are the life-sized statues depicting the Passion and death of Christ, supported shoulder high by men in hooded white robes. The processions can last for hours and it takes six strong men to carry each of the painted statues, with frequent pauses to rest. People dressed as soldiers and Biblical characters also march to the sombre music.

The **Easter Sunday** procession, by contrast, is more of a parade. Usually led by the local band, it is a much happier occasion, with a statue of the risen Christ carried through the streets to the sound of church bells.

**Above:** *Lacemaking is Gozo's best-known home industry.*

A traditional feature of **Christmas** is the illuminated crib displays, some with moving figures, to be found in several of Malta's village churches.

## The Arts

Specialist **Gozitan** craftwork includes lace napkins, handkerchiefs and tablecloths, and cheap and chunky woollen jumpers and cardigans. Village women sit outside their homes in the cool of a summer's evening, chatting and working away with knitting needles or lace-maker's cushions. Durable hand-woven Malta Weave rugs, tablecloths, bedspreads and soft toys are other good buys.

Watercolours by local artists are also excellent value. Among the most popular artists is **Edwin Galea**, painter both of tranquil island landscapes and all-action sea battles depicting Maltese history from the Great Siege to the present day.

---

**Architect Supreme**
**Gerolamo Cassar**
(1520–1586) was Malta's master architect of the 16th century. As assistant to the Pope's engineer Francesco Laparelli, he helped to plan and build Valletta; when Laparelli returned to Italy in 1570, Cassar took charge. His many fine achievements include St John's Co-Cathedral, the Palace of the Grand Masters, the auberges of the Knights, Our Lady of Victories Church and the original Carmelite Church in the capital. He also designed Verdala Palace.

See Map H–C2  ★★★

## ST JOHN'S CO-CATHEDRAL

The façade is plain, even austere; inside it is sumptuous beyond belief. As the Conventual Church of the Knights, it was granted status as Co-Cathedral, together with Mdina's Baroque Cathedral (*see page 23*), by Pope Pius VII in 1816.

The church, dedicated to John the Baptist, is regarded as the finest work of Maltese architect **Gerolamo Cassar** (*see page 13*). It was created between 1573 and 1577.

The barrel-vaulted interior and gilded walls create an overwhelming impression. The oil-painted ceiling, masterpiece of Mattia Preti, depicts 18 episodes in the life of John the Baptist.

Most Grand Masters who served in Malta are buried here. French Grand Masters L'Isle Adam and La Valette are among 12 entombed in the crypt; others occupy ornate Baroque tombs in many of the 12 chapels of the Knights' langues on either side of the nave. Others of Maltese nobility lie buried beneath the marble floor slabs.

The silver gates to the last chapel on the right, the Chapel of the Blessed Sacrament, were painted black in 1798 to conceal their value from the occupying French. The gates, mistaken for iron, were left while other parts of the church were looted. Fine Flemish tapestries, based on works by Rubens and Poussin, are kept in the Cathedral Museum and adorn the nave during the Festival of St John in mid-June.

**St John's Co-Cathedral**
🕐 Masses from 07:30–08:30.
✉ St John Square, St John Street, Valletta.
☎ 21225639.
📠 21454136.
🖱 info@maltachurch.org.mt
💰 Free.

**St John's Museum**
(for Caravaggio paintings, clerical vestments collection, Flemish tapestries):
🕐 09:30–12:50 and 13:30–16:50 Mon–Fri; 09:30–12:50 Sat. Closed on Sundays and public holidays.
✉ St John's Co-Cathedral.
☎ 21220536.
💰 Lm1; children under-15 and students: free.

**Below:** *The plain façade of St John's Co-Cathedral hides a magnificent array of treasures within.*

# CO-CATHEDRAL & GRAND MASTERS' PALACE

See Map H–C2 ★★★

## PALACE OF THE GRAND MASTERS (STATE ROOMS)

The most highly prized of Malta's palaces is now the seat of the President and Parliament of Malta. Every building of the Knights' era was constructed on a grand scale – the palace exceptionally so.

**Above:** *Neptune Court, larger of the two inner court-yards in the Palace of the Grand Masters.*

Malta's supreme architect of the 16th century, **Gerolamo Cassar** was responsible for the building's design and construction in 1571. The palace had started life two years earlier as a house built for Eustachio del Monte, nephew of Italian Grand Master Pietro del Monte. Impressed by the building's focal position on one of the highest points of Mount Sceberras, Del Monte purchased it for the Knights and commissioned Cassar to turn it into a palace.

It was modified by successive Grand Masters until the Order left Malta in 1798. From 1814, it became the British Governor's official residence; since the mid-1970s it has been the President's office.

The palace encloses two courtyards – **Neptune Court**, with its bronze statue of Neptune, and the smaller **Prince Alfred Court** which contains a four-faced clock. The **Tapestry Room** is magnificent, with its superb timbered ceiling and exquisitely preserved Gobelin tapestries. Equally impressive is the Hall of St Michael and St George, also known as the **Throne Room**. Here, too, admire the fine ceiling and the Great Siege frescoes. In the **Hall of the Ambassadors**, a frieze recalls the Knights' pre-Malta history in the eastern Mediterranean.

> **Palace of the Grand Masters**
> ⏰ 1 October–15 June: Mondays, Tuesdays and Wednesdays: 08:30–15:45; Thursdays, Fridays: 08:30–16:00. 16 June–30 September: Mondays–Fridays: 08:00–13:00. Saturdays and Sundays by appointment.
> ✉ Republic Street, Valletta.
> ☎ 21221221.
> 📠 21241241.
> ♿ *See* State-owned museums (page 37).

15

**Above:** *The Auberge de Castile et Leon houses the Prime Minister's office. The statue is of Maltese writer Manuel Dimech (1860–1921).*

See Map H–C1/C2 ★★★

# VALLETTA'S AUBERGES

An *auberge* was the main base of a *langue*, or nationality, of the Knights. There were eight in Valletta but now just five survive.

The **Auberge de Castile et Leon** (ex-British army headquarters now housing the Prime Minister's office) was the palace of the Spanish and Portuguese Knights, built originally by Cassar in 1574 but restyled in 1744 by Domenico Cachia under Grand Master Manuel Pinto de Fonseca.

Down Merchants Street is Cassar's **Auberge d'Italie**, headquarters of the Italian Knights. Built in 1574, it was enlarged in 1683 for Grand Master Gregorio Carafa. Nearby on Republic Street, the Cassar-inspired **Auberge de Provence**, built in 1575, now houses the National Museum of Archaeology (*see* page 37). It was the mansion of France's Provence *langue*. Two other French auberges, the **Auberge de France** and **Auberge d'Auvergne**, were bombed in World War II; the **Auberge d'Allemagne** gave way to St Paul's Anglican Cathedral (*see* page 34).

The final two auberges are near the cathedral. The **Auberge d'Aragon**, a simple single-storey building designed by Cassar on Independence Square, is the oldest auberge, dating from 1571. It now houses the Ministry for Economic Services. The **Auberge de Bavière**, in the former Palace of Bali Carner (1696), housed the Anglo-Bavarian *langue* throughout its existence from 1784–98.

---

**The National Library**
The library contains a wealth of information, including the archives of the Order of St. John – about 7 000 manuscript volumes dating from 1107–1798. Other treasures include the archives of Università, a number of codices and a collection of incunabula.
🕐 1 Oct–15 Jun: 8:15–17:45 Mon–Fri, 8.15–13:15 Sat. 16 Jun–30 Sep: 8:15–13:15 Mon–Sat.
✉ 36 Old Treasury Street, Valletta.
☎ 236585, 243297.
📠 235992.
📧 joseph.boffa@magnet.mt
🖥 http://portico.bl.uk/gabriel/en/countries/malta.html

| See Map H–D1 | ★ ★ ★ |
|---|---|

## THE SACRA INFERMERIA

The Knights' legacy to Malta includes many outstanding buildings, chief among them the **Sacra Infermeria**, or Holy Infirmary. The mighty hospital, high above Grand Harbour, was founded in 1574, soon after the Knights' relocation from Birgu, and was remarkably well-equipped throughout the Knights' stay.

With the French occupation of Malta in 1800, the Sacra Infermeria was looted of the silver plate that financed patient care and became a military hospital, a role it continued to play under the British until 1920. Casualties from the Gallipoli landings were brought here in 1915. Medical history was made in 1887 with the discovery of the brucellosis bacteria by David Bruce.

Four direct hits by World War II bombs reduced parts of the infirmary to rubble. Restoration work, shelved through lack of funds in 1960, resumed in 1974 and the building reopened as the prestigious **Mediterranean Conference Centre** in 1979. The main Republic Hall and adjacent rooms were rebuilt in 1987 after a fire, caused by a laser beam igniting the main stage curtain.

**Knights' Hospital**
The Great Ward of the **Sacra Infermeria**, 155m (170yd) long and 10.5m (34ft) wide, was the world's longest hospital ward. It held 563 beds and could take 914 in times of emergency. Unusually for the time, each patient had a bed to himself with a woollen mattress. Meals for Knights and civilian patients were served on silver plate by the Knights themselves – even the Grand Master fulfilled his obligation to the Order by taking a turn on meal duty.

**Mediterranean Conference Centre**
🕘 Monday–Friday: 09:30–16.30, Saturday: 09:30–12:30, closed on weekends and public holidays.
✉ Mediterranean Street, Valletta.
☎ 21243840.
📠 21245900.
🖐 pr@mcc.com.mt
🖥 www.mcc.com.mt
💰 Lm1 + VAT.
🚌 Conducted tours.
🍽 La Valette.

**Left:** *The Mediterranean Conference Centre successfully blends fine old architecture with modern technology.*

See Map H–C3

★ ★ ★

# GRAND HARBOUR

Arguably the world's greatest natural deep-water harbour, Grand Harbour penetrates inland for nearly 3.5km (2¼ miles) from **St Elmo Point** and **Ricasoli Point** at its entrance to the dockyards of **Marsa Creek**. Focal point of Malta's two great sieges, when it sheltered vast naval fleets, Grand Harbour today sees only limited commercial activity and cruise ships. The cruise traffic is steadily being developed following the building of the cruise terminal below Lascaris Bastion.

From Valletta, looking across Grand Harbour, you can identify (from the left) **Kalkara Creek, Dockyard Creek** and **French Creek** within the promontories of Vittoriosa and Senglea. The **Dockyard**, which employed more than 13,000 men – 15% of Malta's workforce – before Britain's naval withdrawal, now provides work for fewer than 5000, mostly in the ship repair yards.

Grand Harbour is best explored on the 75-minute **Harbour Cruise** that departs several times daily from the Strand at Sliema and also takes in **Marsamxett Harbour** and the creeks of the Three Cities.

**Grand Harbour Cruise**
🕐 Departure: Daily from Sliema Ferries. March and April: 10:30, 11:30, 12:30, 13:15, 14:45. May–November: 10:00, 11:00, 12:15, 13:15, 14:45. ✉ Captain Morgan Cruises, Dolphin Court, Tigne Seafront, Sliema. ☎ 21343373, 21331961. 📠 21332004. ✆ info@captainmorgan.com.mt 💻 www.captainmorgan.com.mt 💰 Adults: Lm6.25; children under-12: Lm4.95.

**Right:** *Grand Harbour is a port of call on a growing number of Mediterranean cruising programmes.*

| ☼ See Map G–A2 | ★ ★ ★ |
|---|---|

## ST JULIAN'S

In summer, this former fishing village at the head of Spinola Bay presents a colourful scene. Brightly painted *luzzu* boats bob in the bay as fishing folk still go about their business – the men unravelling and drying their nets; the women selling the day's catch.

Some of Malta's best restaurants are here, making use of the pair of fine old arched boathouses that once stood like twin sentinels in the grounds of majestic **Spinola Palace**. The palace, built in 1688 by Paolo Rafael Spinola, Grand Prior of Lombardy, is an architectural masterpiece that itself contains a restaurant. A promenade extends the length of the bay towards the prominent Cavalieri Hotel.

**Spinola Bay** is a narrow extension of wider St Julian's Bay; across the bay, on Tower Road leading from Sliema, is **St Julian's Tower**, one of several coastal fortifications erected at the time of Grand Master Martin de Redin in the late 1650s.

**Above:** *Spinola Bay at St Julian's, a popular spot for restaurants, still exudes a fishing village atmosphere.*

**Spinola Palace**
Spinola Palace now houses an elegant restaurant, L-Ghonnella (see page 66).

**St Julian's Tower**
St Julian's Tower has been converted into a simple café, the Torri.

**Eden Leisure Centre**
Includes a tenpin bowling centre, cinemas, Axis Discotheque, the Eden Ice Arena, Cynergi Health & Fitness Club and the the IMAX Vodafone Theatre. 🖥 www.edenleisure.com

See Map I–A1/B1 ★ ★ ★

*Above: Mighty Fort St Angelo was the Knights' headquarters in the Great Siege. It commands the entrance to Grand Harbour.*

## FORT ST ANGELO

This imposing fortress thrusting out into Grand Harbour at the tip of the Vittoriosa peninsula, is an architectural masterpiece. It was built by Grand Master **L'Isle Adam** after the Knights' arrival in 1530. Work involved strengthening an old **Arab** fortification and embracing a mansion of the **De Nava family** and tiny **St Anne's Chapel**, both of which survive.

It became the Knights' headquarters and their command centre during the Great Siege of 1565, when it came under fierce bombardment after the fall of Fort St Elmo across Grand Harbour; its mighty cannon were capable of repelling any seaborne invasion by the Turks. Though restored in the late 17th century, the fort fell into disrepair. Some 350 years after the Knights had made Fort St Angelo their base, it again became a headquarters – this time of the **British Navy**, first as HMS Egmont and from 1933 as HMS St Angelo. In World War II, it suffered some 70 direct hits by bombs. In the mid-1980s it served briefly as a tourist complex.

**Fort St Angelo**
🕐 The lower part is open for visiting on Saturdays 10:00–14:00 (09:00–13:00 in summer). The upper part of the fort is granted to the Order of St John.
✉ Vittoriosa.
💰 Adults: 50c; children (4–16 years old): 25c. Entrance tickets also cover Fort St Elmo (*see page 28*).
🚌 Guided tours of the fort, hourly, between 09:15 and 12:15.

# FORT ST ANGELO, TEMPLES & HYPOGEUM

| See Map D–G4 | ★★★ |

## TARXIEN TEMPLES & HYPOGEUM

**Ħal Saflieni Hypogeum**, Malta's unique underground temple complex, was discovered in 1902 in Paola. It has a labyrinth of corridors and chambers on three levels, cut from the soft limestone 4000–5000 years ago. The upper level, 6m (20ft) below ground, dates from 3000BC; the other two levels, to a depth of 12m (40ft), were built around 2000BC. The latter resemble surface temples elsewhere and so have more ornate features. This was a place of ancient worship and burial and the lowest level contained a burial chamber with the remains of 7000 bodies. The Holy of Holies chamber has strong architectural features and the red colouring of death on its walls – it was probably a shrine for the sacrifice of animals. The oracle chamber has outstanding acoustics and reverberate male – but not female – voices around its walls.

On the southern clifftop between Ghar Lapsi and Blue Grotto are two more prehistoric temple sites. Hagar Qim occupies the higher ground; Mnajdra is lower down.

**Hagar Qim** ('standing stones') used some of the largest slabs found in Maltese temple buildings. The blocks were transported on stone balls, but archaeologists remain baffled as to how the larger ones were raised upright.

**Mnajdra**'s three temples, within their protective coralline limestone wall, are in better condition than Hagar Qim. The temples, dating from 2500BC, feature good corbelling and decorative work.

**Ħal Saflieni Hypogeum**
🕐 1 October – 15 June: 08:45, 09:45, 10:45, 11:45, 13:45, 14:45, 15:45. 16 June – 30 September: every hour 08:15–12:00. Tickets are purchased from site; may be purchased up to 15 days in advance; often a long waiting list.
✉ Ħal Saflieni Street, Paola.
☎ 21825579.
📠 21805021.
🖥 museumsinfo@magnet.mt
💻 www.magnet.mt/home/museums
💰 Adults: Lm3; under-19 and senior citizens: Lm1.

**Tarxien Temples**
🕐 *See* State-owned museums, page 37.
✉ Neolithic Temples Street, Tarxien.
☎ 21695578.
💰 Adults: Lm1; under-19 and over 65: free.

**Below:** *An aerial view of the Mnajdra temple site clearly shows the shape of the three temples.*

⊙ See Map D–F6

★ ★ ★

## BLUE GROTTO

**Blue Grotto**
🕐 April–October. Boat trips run daily, weather permitting; there are no specific times.
✉ Wied-iż-Żurrieq.
☎ 21640058.
💰 Boat trips to the system of caverns: Adults Lm2.50, children Lm1.25.

Malta's rugged southern coast is pitted with sea caves, of which the Blue Grotto is the most spectacular. The 25-minute boat trip is best enjoyed in the early morning, when shafts of bright sunlight reflecting inside the cave turn the water several shades of vivid blue. Weather permitting, small boats holding up to eight passengers leave the rocky inlet by the fishing hamlet of **Wied-iż-Żurrieq**, with its handful of cafés and souvenir shops at the bottom of a scenic road from Żurrieq Village.

Though it sounds inviting, the Blue Grotto is inaccessible for swimming. It is however a fairly popular dive site. Across the bay, along the cliff wall, an underwater cave is situated at 23m (76ft). A larger cave is around the corner at a similar depth. The caves and algae beds contain interesting marine life such as tube worms, peacock worms, cuttlefish and wrasse.

**Below:** *An excursion boat enjoys calm weather to explore the Blue Grotto.*

See Map E–C1    ★ ★ ★

## MDINA'S BAROQUE CATHEDRAL

Mdina's Baroque cathedral is dedicated to St Paul and shares the title of Co-Cathedral with St John's in Valletta. It was erected between 1697 and 1702 after the 1693 earthquake had all but destroyed the 13th-century original. The Maltese architect **Lorenzo Gafa** designed the new building that was to prove his masterpiece.

Within the grand and gilded interior, the marble floor tablets identify the graves of important social and religious figures. The apse, survivor of the earthquake with its 'Shipwreck of St Paul' mural by Mattia Preti, found a place in the new cathedral; also saved from the earthquake were the marble font and oak sacristy door.

**Above:** *The clock and bell tower on the cathedral.*

The cathedral's striking dome – a readily recognizable feature of the Mdina skyline – is widely regarded as Gafa's finest work. The inside of the dome was painted by **Mario Caffaro Rore** in 1955.

Fine decorations include the nave ceiling fresco of 1794 by two Sicilian brothers, **Antonio** and **Vincenzo Manno**, depicting the life of St Paul. Other treasures are the Madonna icon, which some take to be the work of St Luke; a silver medieval cross believed to have been brought by the Knights from Rhodes; and a communion chalice supposedly used by St Paul. The two early-17th century bronze cannons formally guarding the cathedral's entrance, were returned from London at the insistence of the Governor in 1888.

**Cathedral**
🕐 Masses from 04:00–17:30.
✉ St Paul's Square, Mdina.
☎ 21456620.
📠 21454136.
📧 info@maltachurch.org.mt
💰 Free.
🚌 No guided tours.

**Cathedral Museum**
🕐 09:00–16:30 Mon–Fri and 09:00–14:00 Sat. Closed on Sundays and public holidays.
✉ Archbishop Square, Mdina.
☎ 21454697.
📠 21450455.
💰 Museum: Lm1.
🚌 No guided tours.

| ⊙ See Map F–A3 | ★ ★ ★ |
|---|---|

**Right:** *St Paul's Catacombs, largest of Rabat's ancient burial complexes.*

## RABAT'S CATACOMBS

Rabat has a vast network of catacombs and two in St Agatha Street are open to visitors. The most extensive, **St Paul's Catacombs**, are a labyrinth of tunnels, niches and rock tombs said to date from the 4th and 5th centuries. **St Agatha's Catacombs** are below the church dedicated to the saint, who fled to Malta from Catania in AD249 to escape persecution and is believed to have hidden in the underground cemetery before returning to Sicily to die a martyr.

As their belief that the dead should be buried conflicted with Roman law stipulating cremation, Malta's Christians adopted the burial method of the Palestinian Jews by carving these vast labyrinths. Family graves are cut into the rock walls; there are also stone canopies, benches and communion tables used by the early Christians. Just visible on some tombs are the remains of frescoes.

---

**St Paul's Catacombs**
⊙ *See* State museums, page 37. Closed on public holidays.
✉ St Agatha Street, Rabat.
☎ 21454125.
🎫 Adults: Lm1; under-19 and over-65: free.

**St Agatha's Catacombs**
⊙ Oct–June: 09:00–12:00 and 13:00–17.00 Mon–Fri. July–Sept: 09:00–17.00 Mon–Fri; 09:00–13.00 Sat. Closed Sundays and public holidays.
✉ St Agatha Street, Rabat.
☎ 21454503.
📠 21450196.
🎫 50c.

See Map A–A1/B1  ★ ★ ★

## VICTORIA'S CITADEL

Gozo island suffered severely at the hands of the Turks and other marauding raiders throughout the Middle Ages and the only solution appeared to be the construction of a city stronghold in which the population could gather in times of danger. The mighty bastions you see today, built around 1600 and funded jointly by King Philip II of Spain and the Gozitans themselves, were never put to the test. By that time the Turks had fled back east, leaving the Gozitans in relative peace – though spasmodic raids occurred into the 18th century.

In 1637 a law requiring all islanders to sleep within the Citadel was rescinded; the people moved out and thus began the decline of the old city's importance. Many of the vacated buildings within those walls were destroyed by the 1693 earthquake. Today the towering ramparts embrace the cathedral, a number of museums, some craft shops and the crumbled medieval dwellings that are now the subject of a restoration programme. Do not leave the Citadel without walking round the ramparts; the 360-degree panorama that unfolds before your eyes offers the best views of Gozo.

**Victoria's Citadel**
✉ Victoria Local Council, Banca Giuratale, Independence Square, Victoria, Gozo.
☎ 21563344.
📞 21563355.
💰 Free except for museums.
🚍 No specific guided tours, though Gozo excursions usually take in the Citadel.

**Below:** *Stepped alleyway in Victoria's Citadel, part of a maze of passages within the fortified walls.*

**Mosta Dome**
🕐 Masses from 05:00–17:00.
✉ Rotunda Square, Mosta.
☎ 21433826.
📠 21418368.
💰 Free.

✿ See Map D–D4    ★ ★ ★

## MOSTA DOME

The buzzing little town of Mosta is best known for the **Church of St Mary**, usually called simply either the **Mosta Dome** or the **Rotunda**, and visible from a large part of the island. At 37m (122ft) across, it is Europe's third largest unsupported dome, built between 1833 and 1860 in the style of the Pantheon and surpassed in size only by St Peter's in Rome and St Sophia's in Istanbul. Taller, but slightly narrower, is the St John's Church at Xewkija in Gozo.

The Rotunda was built by volunteer labour, completed without the use of scaffolding and financed entirely by the local parish. On display is the casting of the World War II bomb that fell through the roof and rolled across the floor during a service, but miraculously failed to explode. Just west of Mosta is the **Chapel of Tal L'Isperanza**, typical of the tiny wayside chapels found in more remote parts of the Maltese countryside.

**Below:** *The Classical frontage of the Rotunda in Mosta.*

⚙ See Map B–C2    ★ ★ ★

## ĠGANTIJA TEMPLES

The largest and best preserved of the islands' prehistoric temple sites, Ġgantija in Gozo is claimed to be the world's oldest free-standing structure – older even than the Egyptian pyramids or Stonehenge in Britain. According to legend, the massive blocks of Ġgantija (the word means 'gigantic') were carried from Ta' Ċenċ in the south of the island by a female giant, some time between 3600 and 3000BC. Some are as much as 6m (20ft) high and weigh many tonnes.

The complex, on a fenced-in hilltop site a few minutes' walk from the centre of Xagħra, was unearthed in 1827 and comprises two temples, built several centuries apart, with a forecourt. Each temple has five lobe-shaped apses leading off a central corridor; features within are the floor libation holes, limestone blocks with spiral decoration, an oracle hole and a stone recess for washing feet. The large altar blocks were almost certainly used for the sacrifice of animals.

**Above:** *The ancient structures at Ġgantija, most impressive of Malta and Gozo's temple sites.*

> **Ġgantija Temples**
> 🕐 08:30–16:30 Mon–Sat; 08:30–15:00 Sunday year-round.
> ✉ Xagħra plateau, Xagħra.
> ☎ 21553194.
> 💰 Adults: Lm1 (the ticket is also valid for the Ta' Kola Windmill (see page 82); under-19 and over-65: free.

See Map H–D1    ★ ★

## THE FORTIFICATIONS

Arriving in Malta by sea, the first landmark you pass entering Grand Harbour is star-shaped **Fort St Elmo** on the exposed tip of the Valletta peninsula. Under massive bombardment, it defied the Turks for 31 days in the Great Siege of 1565. The fort was rebuilt in 1567 and has since been strengthened and enlarged by the Knights and the British; it now houses the National War Museum.

Leading out to Fort St Elmo on both sides of the tiny peninsula are the mighty **curtain walls** behind which Valletta took shape. On the landward side, now separating Valletta from its suburb of Floriana, the defences are strengthened by four mighty **bastions** and are further protected by a wide moat 18m (60ft) deep.

The City Gate entrance cuts through the curtain wall between **St John's Cavalier** and **St James Cavalier**; in all, 11 bastions ring the city. Sections of wall are still known by the *langues* of the Knights which protected them – French, English and German Curtain. All around the peninsula, are stunning views out to sea or across the two great harbours; below **St Salvatore Bastion** on the Marsamxett side is the **Manderaggio**, a sheltered inlet used by the Knights.

**Fort St Elmo**
🕐 Sat 13:00–17:00;
Sun 09:00–17:00.
Closed: Mon–Fri and
public holidays.
✉ St Elmo Street,
Valletta.
☎ 21222430.
💰 Adults: 50c;
children (aged 4–16):
25c; includes entrance
to Fort St Angelo.
🚌 Guided tours of
Fort St Elmo start at 15
minutes past the hour.

**National War Museum**
🕐 *See* State museums,
page 37. Closed on
public holidays.
✉ St Elmo Street,
Valletta.
☎ 21222430.
💰 Adults:Lm1; under-
19 and over-65: free.

# THE FORTIFICATIONS & GĦAR DALAM

| ☼ See Map D–G5 | ★ ★ |
| --- | --- |

## GĦAR DALAM

Many of the dwarf elephant and hip-popotamus that roamed 130,000 years ago over what is now Malta, ended up in this long, tapering cave on the side of a dry river valley above **Birżebbuġa**.

Excavations that started in 1865 have uncovered enough to fill every case in the small museum at the cave's entrance, including elephant molars, deer bones, antlers and hippo teeth. Their discovery fuelled speculation that the Maltese islands were once part of a land bridge between Europe and Africa. Thousands of animals would have perished in the Stone Age cave, with the carcasses of many others washed there by floodwater. Some stumps of stalactites and stalagmites have survived and five distinct geological layers can be identified from the side-lit visitors' walkway running the length of the cave. Recent evidence indicates that the cave was used by Bronze Age man and later by the Phoenicians.

> **Għar Dalam and Museum**
> ⊕ See State museums, page 37; closed on public holidays.
> ⊠ Zejtun Road, Birżebbuġia.
> ☎ 21675419.
> 💰 Adults: Lm1; under-19 and over-65: free.

**Opposite:** *St Barbara Bastion and Barriera Wharf form part of the imposing fortifications along Valletta's Grand Harbour shore.*
**Below:** *Exploring the depths of Għar Dalam, the 'cave of darkness'.*

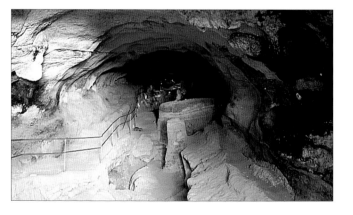

See Map I–A3 ★★

**Fort St Rocco**
🕐 Daily 10:00–16:00, closed on public holidays.
✉ Limits of Kalkara.
🏆 Adults: 50 cents.
🚌 Every Saturday and Sunday there is a live re-enactment of Victorian Garrison.

## COTONERA LINES

The town of Cospicua, known as Bormla when it absorbed the overflow populace from the Knights' fortified base of Birgu, today links Senglea and Vittoriosa. The town's clustered streets nestle inside a double ring of bastions built to protect the Three Cities from land attack.

It was in the mid-16th century that Bormla's growth called for new defences and in 1639 the Margherita Lines began to take shape. Six bastions were planned; three were completed quickly and the others by the 1730s. Work was interrupted when Grand Master **Nicolas Cotoner** pledged to fund an even stronger fortification and between 1670 and 1680, the Cotonera Lines were built, their eight mighty bastions and two demi-bastions strengthening 5km (3 miles) of defences and offering protection for 40,000 people and their animals. Included in the scheme was the construction of **Fort Ricasoli**.

**Below:** *Żabbar Gate, the impressive and ornate entrance to the Three Cities.*

The defences were never tested – with a garrison of 8000 at the time of the French invasion in 1798, the Knights would have been hard-pressed to defend the Lines – and Bormla never grew to fill the enclosed area. Entry into the Three Cities was then, as now, through ornate gateways; impressive still is **Żabbar Gate**, a towering flag-adorned archway on the road from Żabbar, bearing a bronze bust of Grand Master Nicolas Cotoner.

See Map D–D5/D6 ★ ★

## BUSKETT GARDENS AND VERDALA PALACE

Buskett Gardens consist of a delightfully green area which is the last vestige of the forest that once covered Malta. It is popular for its flora in spring and its wooded shade in summer. The name stems from the Italian *boschetto* (little wood). In late June, crowds gather here for the **Mnarja** festival.

Overlooking the lush greenery of Buskett Gardens, Verdala Palace was built in 1586 as a luxurious summer retreat for extrovert French cardinal Grand Master Hugues Loubenx de Verdalle. It was designed by Gerolamo Cassar as a fortified castle and today, as the official summer residence of the President of the Republic of Malta, it is used to host visiting VIPs. A flight of steps crosses the moat from which was cut the palace's building stone; inside a superb elliptical staircase in one corner leads to the first floor. The great hall contains frescoes of Verdalle's life, while in the first-floor dining room is the chess board chiselled out of the stone floor by French prisoners in 1812.

**Above:** *Verdala Palace overlooks the verdant Buskett Gardens, with their plantations of firs, cypress, oaks and citrus trees.*

**Buskett Gardens**
- ⊕ 07:00–18:00.
- ✉ Buskett Forest, limits of Rabat.
- ☎ 21493170/1.
- ⎙ 21493176.
- 🛈 Free.

**Verdala Palace**
- ⊕ The palace is not open to the public.
- ✉ Buskett Forest, limits of Rabat.

| See Map D | ★★ |

*Above: Crowded beach umbrellas provide a colourful contrast to sand and sky at Golden Bay.*

---

**BEACHES IN MALTA**

**Mellieħa Bay**
Location: Map D–B2
Closest town: Mellieħa

**Golden Bay**
Location: Map D–B3
Closest town: Għajn Tuffieħa

**Għajn Tuffieħa Bay**
Location: Map D–B3
Closest town: Għajn Tuffieħa

**Għejna Bay**
Location: Map D–B4
Closest town: Mġarr

---

## Malta's Beaches

**Mellieħa Bay** is Malta's largest beach, 600m (⅓ mile) long and resplendent with bright umbrellas in summer, when it throngs with people. It is excellent for swimming, sunbathing and water ports – dinghies, pedaloes and windsurfers are available. There are also a couple of no-frills beach cafés.

**Golden Bay** lives up to its name, with fine yellow sand and a range of water sports. As it can become crowded in high season, a good time to visit is late afternoon, when the crowds start to thin out.

**Għajn Tuffieħa Bay** is situated next to Golden Bay. The name means 'eye of the apple' and it is even prettier than Golden Bay. Situated below a long flight of steps starting from beside the long-redundant Riviera Martinique Hotel, it is quiet without being secluded and is excellent for bathing. Both Golden Bay and Għajn Tuffieħa Bay can be reached by bus from Valletta.

**Għejna Bay** (translates as 'small garden') is popular with the locals. It is a small beach with a neat line of boathouses cut into the limestone cliff. It has limited facilities but offers peace and quiet. The bay is signposted west of Mġarr through the green Għejna Valley.

See Map B  ★ ★

## Gozo's Beaches

**Ramla Bay** is Gozo's one real sandy beach, with sand as golden as you will find anywhere and the water inviting, though care must be exercised because of currents. The beach is generally less crowded than those in Malta, even on the hottest days.

**Marsalforn** is Gozo's chief holiday resort. The whole seafront area has been recently redesigned, with better paving along the promenade and the short sand and shingle beach improved. A short distance to the west, at the foot of the narrow road from Żebbuġ, are the bays of Xwieni and Qbajjar, both good for swimming.

A delightful little seaside village, **Xlendi** has maintained its appeal as Gozo's second resort to Marsalforn. Small boats bob in front of the narrow sandy beach, sheltered by tall cliffs and guarded by the Xlendi Tower.

One of the most scenically attractive little beaches of the islands is at **San Blas Bay** in Gozo. Follow the sign out of Nadur to the bay and take the single-track road downwards. A surfaced footpath leads down past cultivated terraces to the tiny sandy bay. It is one of the truly peaceful spots on the planet.

Another small beach at the eastern end of Gozo is at **Hondoq Bay**. The road east from Qala winds down to the usually deserted sandy inlet, where the water takes on a brilliant turquoise appearance to rival that of Comino's **Blue Lagoon** (see page 81).

---

**BEACHES IN GOZO**
**Ramla Bay**
Location: Map B–C1

**Marsalforn**
Location: Map B–B1

**Xlendi**
Location: Map B–B3

**San Blas Bay**
Location: Map B–C1

**Hondoq Bay**
Location: Map B–D2

---

**COMINO'S BEACH**
**Blue Lagoon**
Location: Map D–A1
(West side of the island).

---

**Below:** *Tiny Xlendi at the head of its landlocked bay. The calm water in the bay is ideal for swimming.*

**Above:** *St Paul Shipwreck Church recalls the Apostle's arrival in Malta in* AD60.

---

**St Paul in Malta**

St Paul and his fellow prisoners were welcomed ashore after their shipwreck. The **Church of St Paul** in San Pawl Il Baħar is said to be on the site where St Paul shook off a deadly viper into the fire and won over the islanders. The spring of **Għajn Razul**, or **Apostle's Fountain**, is supposedly where St Paul struck a rock to provide drinking water for the survivors. St Paul spent three months in Malta, preaching the Gospel (he converted the Roman governor Publius to Christianity) and healing the sick, before continuing his journey via Syracuse to Rome.

---

# Churches and Cathedrals

## St Paul Shipwreck Church, Valletta

This was one of Valletta's first churches and commemorates St Paul's arrival in Malta in AD60. The painted and gilded wooden figure of the apostle by Maltese sculptor Melchiore Gafa which stands to the left of the altar, is carried through Valletta each year on the saint's feast day, 10 February. The church contains one of St Paul's arm bones and a section of the column on which he was beheaded; it also possesses a prized silver collection.

✉ 74 St Paul's Street, Valletta, ☎21223348, 📠 21236013, ⏱ Masses from 07:00–18:00.

## St Paul's Anglican Cathedral, Valletta

Also dedicated to St Paul, the neoclassical cathedral, with its 65m (210ft) spire, shapes Valletta's skyline. It was built in 1844 and funded by the Dowager Queen Adelaide.

✉ Archbishop Street, Valletta, ☎ 21225714.

## St Publius Church, Floriana

Built between 1733 and 1768, this church was named after the Roman governor whom St Paul converted to Christianity in AD60. It was the last parish church built by the Knights.

✉ 4 Sarria Street, Floriana, ☎ 21247106.

## Church of St Lawrence, Vittoriosa

This grand building is a 1691 reconstruction by Maltese architect Lorenzo Gafa of the former 16th-century Knights' Conventual Church. It has a rich marbled interior, with well-lit side chapels and paintings of the saint.

✉ 91 St Lawrence Street, Vittoriosa, ☎ 21827057, 📠 21667664, ⏱ Masses from 06:00–18:00.

## Church of St Helena, Birkirkara

The shining glory of Birkirkara is this tall Baroque parish church, designed by Maltese architect Domenico Cachia and built between 1735 and 1745. The external features include two attractive bell towers; the interior is richly gilded and carved, with excellent frescoes.
☒ *4 Sanctuary Street, B'Kara,* ☎ *21444725.*

## Victoria's Cathedral

The cathedral was started in 1697 and completed in 1711. While the outside may lack the ornamentation of other Maltese churches, the inside is far from plain. Once inside look skywards for the interior's focal point, the beautifully proportioned painting of the 1730s by Italian artist Antonio Manuele – a *trompe l'oeil* which gives the illusion of a dome. The roof is actually flat, funds having run short before its completion.

☒ *Cathedral Place, Rabat, Gozo,* ☎ *21554101 (cathedral), 21556087 (museum),* ♬ *21564572 (cathedral),* ☻ *Mon–Sat: 10:00 to 16:30; closed Sundays and public holidays (museum).*

## St George's Basilica, Victoria

This basilica, traditionally Gozo's first parish church, was built in the 1670s and has been beautified over the years; fine artistic works inside include Mattia Preti's painting of St George with his foot victoriously placed on the head of the dragon.
☒ *St George Square, Victoria,* ☎ *21556377,* ♬ *21556981,* ✆ *sangorg@vol.net.mt* ▣ *www. stgeorge.org.net*

### Twin-Tower Style
The twin towers of **St John's Co-Cathedral** in Valletta (*see page 14*), a revolutionary architectural style for mid-16th century Malta that probably derived from Spain, set the pattern for church building in the Maltese islands. There are more than 350 churches and chapels throughout the Maltese islands. Many larger churches have a clock on each tower, one a working timepiece and the other painted on – in the firm belief that this would confuse the devil.

**Below:** *Victoria's cathedral and the remains of medieval houses within the Citadel, whose walls were built nearly 400 years ago as a refuge against the Turks.*

## Malta's Forts
Two forts guard the narrow entrance to Grand Harbour – **Fort St Elmo** (see page 28) at the tip of Valletta and **Fort Ricasoli** (see page 30) just north of Kalkara on the Three Cities side. Fort Ricasoli was built in 1670 by Italian **Antonio Valperga**, responsible for the Cotonera Lines. Under the Knights, it held a 2000-strong garrison – it is now disappointingly used as an oil storage facility but there are plans to remove the oil tanks. A short distance away is **Fort St Rocco** (see page 30), one of a number of smaller coastal defences erected by the Knights.

# Interesting Buildings

## Lascaris War Rooms, Valletta

Also known as the Malta Command Centre, this true-to-life museum was the nerve centre of Allied operations in the Mediterranean during World War II. Life-size figures are seen at work in the various chambers; each scene is frozen from a particular phase of the war.

⊠ Lascaris Ditch, Valletta, ☎ 21238396, ⏱ Mon–Fri 09:30–16:00, Sat–Sun 09:30–12:30, 💰 Adults: Lm1.75, children: 85c.

## Casa Rocca Piccola, Valletta

This house was erected for the Knights' Italian *langue* around 1580, and over the years became home to many Knights before being sold to Maltese nobility in 1784. Today, the De Piro family have an apartment here. It is the only historic Valletta house open to the public.

⊠ 74 Republic Street, Valletta, ☎ 21231796, 📠 21243907, 🖳 www.vol.net.mt/casarocca 💰 Adults: Lm 2.00, children and students: Lm 1.00, 🚌 Guided tours: 10:00, 11:00, 12:00, 13:00, 14:00, 15:00 and 16:00, except Sundays and public holidays.

## Inquisitor's Palace, Vittoriosa

The Inquisition existed to defend the Catholic faith. As the Pope's agent, the Inquisitor was stylishly housed in this palace, which was built around 1574.

⊠ Triq il-Mina il-Kbira, Vittoriosa, ☎ 21663731, ⏱ See State-owned museums (opposite), closed on public holidays. 💰 Adults: Lm1, under-19 and over-65: free.

**Below:** *Carriage of the Inquisitor displayed in the Inquisitor's Palace.*

## Museums and Galleries

### National Museum of Archaeology, Valletta

The museum contains a priceless collection of artefacts saved from prehistoric temple and tomb sites throughout the islands. It does a fine job displaying pottery, sculpted temple stones, figurines, weapons and jewellery. Of particular note are the sculpted Copper Age blocks from Tarxien with their spiral motifs – these are the originals; those at the temple are copies. Watercolours show the temples as they would have appeared and there are detailed models of the prehistoric sites.

✉ *Auberge de Provence, Republic Street, Valletta,* ☎ *21221623 or 21230711,* 🖷 *21243628,* ⏱ *See State museum hours (side panel), closed on public holidays,* 🔸 *Adults: Lm1, under-19 and over-65: free.*

### The Armoury, Valletta

One of the world's most significant and impressive permanent exhibitions of pre-18th century weaponry and armour is found in two halls within the Grand Masters' Palace. The most recent weapons are North European air guns from 1800. A group of armour-clad model Knights stand on parade among the display of guns, swords, rapiers, daggers, pikes, lances and other weapons.

✉ *Palace of the Grand Masters (see page 15).*

### National Museum of Fine Arts, Valletta

Recognized for its impressive assembly

**Above:** *Knights on parade in the Armoury. The fine collection of weaponry and armour numbers some 6000 pieces.*

---

**State-Owned Museums**

⏱ The opening times of the government-run museums vary between winter (1 October to 15 June) and summer (16 June to 30 September). In winter, opening hours are 08:15–17:00 Monday–Saturday and 08:15–16:15 on Sunday. In summer, museums are open daily (including Sunday) from 07:45–14:00. Gozo's museums open from 08:30–16:30 and until 15:00 on Sunday, year-round.

🔸 Admission costs Lm1 for adults; under-19's and over 65's are free. If in doubt, phone the government's Museum Department on ☎ 21230711, 21233821 or 21251874 for opening times.

# SIGHTSEEING

**Above:** *The Maritime Museum with its elegant clock tower beside Dockyard Creek. Historic vessels line the quay.*

---

**Norman House**
On Villegaignon Street, Mdina, near the Carmelite Church, is the restored **Palazzo Falzon**, with a slit-windowed lower section which dates from the 14th century. Sometimes called the **Norman House**, it is the only private house in Mdina open to the public and functions as a museum with a good display of antiques, paintings and furniture.

---

of both Maltese and foreign paintings from the 14th century to the present day, this collection includes work by Mattia Preti, whose masterpiece was the ceiling of St John's Co-Cathedral, the 18th-century artist Antoine de Favray and 17th-century painter Guido Reni.

⊠ *Admiralty House, South Street, Valletta,* ☎ *21233034,* ⌚ *See State-owned museum hours (page 37), closed on public holidays.*
🛈 *Adults: Lm1, under-19 and over-65: free.*

## Maritime Museum, Vittoriosa

Malta's remarkable seafaring heritage long called out for such a museum. The

building, the Royal Naval bakery, was designed by naval architect **William Scamp** in 1842 and has a distinctive clock tower. Vacated by the Navy in 1979, it became a museum in 1992 and includes sections highlighting the Knights, Royal Navy and merchant navy.

⊠ *The Waterfront, Vittoriosa,* ☎ *21660052,* ⌚ *See State-owned museum hours (page 37), closed on public holidays.*
🛈 *Adults: Lm1, under-19 and over-65: free.*

## Mdina's Cathedral Museum

Many artefacts salvaged after the earthquake are on display in this museum, which is housed in the seminary across Archbishop Square to the right of the cathedral. The building is attributed to both Giovanni Barbara and Andrea Belli and dates from 1733. In the museum are silver statues, outstanding Dürer

engravings, paintings, manuscripts, lace and some 15th-century Sicilian choir panels.
⊠ *Archbishop Square, Mdina,*
☎ *21454697,*
⊕ *09:00–16:30 Mon–Fri, closed on Sundays and public holidays.*

## Roman Villa and Museum, Rabat

At the far end of Howard Gardens in Rabat, by the Greeks' Gate leading into Mdina, a small neoclassical museum encloses the mosaic floor of a Roman villa and displays other Roman antiquities. The remains of the villa, among Malta's most significant Roman legacies and probably the home of a wealthy merchant, were discovered in 1881.
⊠ *Museum Square, Rabat,* ☎ *21454125,*
⊕ *Mon–Sat: 08:30–16:30, Sun: 08:30–15:30, closed on public holidays.*
ð *Adults: Lm1, under-19 and over-65: free.*

## Folklore Museum

Gozo life is recounted down the years in displays occupying three medieval houses.
⊠ *Milite Bernardo Street, The Citadel, Victoria,* ☎ *21556144,*
✆ *21559008,* ⊕ *See State-owned museum hours (page 37), closed on public holidays.*
ð *Adults: Lm1, under-19 and over-65: free.*

## Natural Science Museum, Victoria

This museum identifies Gozo's flora and fauna and has a section on the marine environment.
⊠ *Fosse Street, The Citadel, Victoria,*
☎ *21556153,* ⊕ *See State-owned museum hours (page 37), closed on public holidays.*
ð *Adults: Lm1, under-19 and over-65: free.*

---

**Gozo Heritage**
Gozo's 7000-year history is recalled in Gozo Heritage, a series of tableaux housed in a typical Gozitan farmhouse on the Victoria road just outside the village of **Ghajnsielem** (open daily, 10:00–17:00). Animated life-size figures in period costume recall historical scenes, from the legend of Calypso via the culture of the Phoenicians, Romans, Arabs, Normans, early Christians and the Knights. Gozo's part in the Great Siege of 1565 is recounted, as are the influences of Napoleon and Nelson. Its role in World War II is also portrayed.

---

**Below:** *Outstanding example of mosaic work in the Roman Villa and Museum at Rabat. A Roman town flourished in the vicinity.*

# SIGHTSEEING

### San Anton

The Three Villages (Lija, Balzan and Attard) are grouped around the lush greenery of **San Anton Gardens**, next to the Presidential Palace. The gardens, planned in the 17th century, provide a shady retreat in summer and contain some unusual species. There is also a small zoo. The grand house close to Attard, of which the San Anton Gardens form part, is now the official residence of Malta's President. It was built in 1625 as the country retreat of Grand Master **Antoine de Paul**, who found Verdala Palace too far from Valletta for his liking and is said to have upset the Inquisitor by staging a lavish banquet on his first night there. Formerly the Governor's residence, the palace is not open to the public.

**Below:** *The Upper Barracca Gardens at Grand Harbour.*

## Parks and Gardens

### Barracca Gardens, Valletta

Two minutes' walk from the Auberge de Castile et Leon in Valletta are the **Upper Barracca Gardens**, a 17th-century parade ground of the Italian Knights with spectacular harbour views. The **Lower Barracca Gardens**, at the bottom of St Christopher Street, enclose a small Grecian temple monument. To the left when you enter Valletta through City Gate is **Hastings Garden**, named after the Marquis of Hastings.
✉ *1st Ursula Street, Valletta.*
🕐 *07:00–18:00,* 🖰
*valletta.lc@magnet.mt*
💰 *free.*

### Maglio Gardens, Floriana

Beyond the le Meridien Phoenicia Hotel and Independence monument are the tree-lined Maglio Gardens, once an exercise ground of the Knights, with statues of Maltese worthies.
✉ *The Mall, Floriana.*

### The Argotti Botanical Gardens, Floriana

These gardens, created in 1774, are packed with unusual trees and plants from all over the world.
✉ *Vincenzo Bugeja Street, Floriana.*

### Gardjola Garden, Senglea

At Senglea's furthest point, a delightful garden affords the finest views of Valletta. To your right is Fort St Angelo; to your left, the derricks of Marsa; and directly across the water, the bastions that rise to the Upper Barracca Gardens.
✉ *Fort St Michael, Senglea.*

## ACTIVITIES
## Sport and Recreation

There are plenty of sports to occupy the visitor, including **golf** at the par-68, 5091m (5567yd) Royal Malta Golf Club (*see* side panel) and **tenpin bowling** at the computerized Eden Super Bowl in St George's Bay (*see* Eden Leisure Centre, page 19). Runners may want to participate in the **Malta Marathon** which is held each February. Increasingly, tennis and squash courts are found in hotels, as are fitness centres.

The extensive Marsa Sports Club (*see* side panel) offers weekly or daily membership to visitors and includes **tennis**, **squash**, **mini-golf**, **billiards** and **swimming**.

The informal game of *bocci* – like the French boules but using a combination of balls and coloured wooden blocks – is a national pastime. Football is popular in Malta and top foreign teams have a strong following (*see* page 76).

Malta and Gozo are renowned for their water sports. The clear waters and abundant marine life make the islands one of the top diving destinations in the Mediterranean (*see* diving excursions on page 78). Around the resorts, there are plenty of places with boats and water sports equipment for hire and sheltered bays in which to **sail**, **windsurf** and **waterski**. Maltese teams do well at water polo, which is also a popular spectator sport

**Royal Malta Golf Club**
✉ Aldo Moro Street, Marsa, Malta.
☎ 21239302.
📠 21227020.
🖑 info@maltagolf.org
🖥 www.maltagolf.org
🕐 The course is open to visitors every day of the week except for Thursday and Saturday mornings.

**Marsa Sports Club**
✉ Aldo Moro Street, Marsa, Malta.
☎ 21233851 / 21232842.
📠 21231809.
🖑 info@ marsasportsclub.com
🖥 www. marsasportsclub.com
💰 Day membership: Lm2, weekly: Lm10, monthly: Lm30.

**Below:** *A summer evening's* bocci *game at Buġibba. Towns and villages throughout Malta have their own* bocci *clubs (see page 76).*

(*see* page 76). **Fishing** is possible either off the rocky foreshore or by arrangement with a local boatman.

## Alternative Malta

There is an ever-changing number of bars and cafés that are particularly popular with the gay and lesbian community. The Tom Bar and the Lady Godiva Bar are two of the more familiar ones.

**Lady Godiva Bar** is situated in St Julian's, one of the most lively areas of Malta. Due to regulations on the island, Lady Godiva cannot be called an exclusive gay bar, but an exclusively male bar is permitted by law. Decorated by local designers, the bar is dark in colour with candles scattered all over the bar area. Theme nights are held on most weekends and include drag nights, leather nights and 80's and 90's nights. Cabaret is usually on Saturday and the bar is frequented by the 'in crowd' of the island. Although considered an exclusive gay bar, a mixed crowd can be found in the bar as long as they are gay-friendly.

The **Tom Bar** is situated just outside Valletta. On two floors overlooking Grand Harbour, the 300-year-old building is believed to have been a tax office for the Knights of Malta until 1798. Later, this intriguingly located venue by the port survived the poundings of World War II only to become a bar and brothel quite soon afterwards.

The **Hotel Kappara** in Kappara has a discreet, friendly and homely atmosphere, a good restaurant and bar, and caters exclusively for gay men.

**Lady Godiva Bar**
✉ Triq il-Wilga, St Julian's.

**Tom Bar**
✉ 1 Crucifix Hill, Floriana.
☎ 21250780.
📠 21316773.
✆ tom@onvol.net
🖥 www.geocities.com/tombarmalta
🕐 Open every evening from 20:30 onwards. Opens 11:30–14:30 for light lunches (Oct–Mar).

**Hotel Kappara**
✉ Triq Wied Ghollieqa, Kappara.
☎ 21334367.
📠 21341281.
✆ kappara@onvol.net
🖥 www.kappara.freeola.com

**More information:**
🖥 www.geocities.com/WestHollywood/Village/3619/
🖥 www.maltagayrights.com

## Fun for Children

Malta has a lot to offer children. There are easily accessible **beaches** (*see* page 32) with safe swimming and facilities. Here you may want to have a seaside picnic, build sandcastles, hire pedallos or try snorkelling. For more fun and entertainment, try the **Christmas pantomime** at the Manoel Theatre (*see* page 71), or a **musical** at the Mediterranean Conference Centre (*see* page 17). In February, join in the **carnival** and in summer, there are **festas** and a programme of street events and fun. The San Anton Gardens (*see* page 40) have a mini **zoo** with a few animals and birds.

**Popeye Village, Anchor Bay, Mellieħa.**
Whether or not you saw the 1980 film *Popeye*, the film set at Anchor Bay is a real treat. The 17 painted wooden water's-edge houses of tumble-down Sweethaven have been refurbished after threatening for years to collapse through neglect. The Paramount film by Robert Altman starred Robin Williams as Popeye and Shelley Duvall as Olive Oyl and is available on video. A cinema by the entrance shows a film about the making of Sweethaven. The price includes entrance to the film set, a 15-minute boat trip, 20 minutes of history about the film set at the cinema and animation shows every hour. There is also a fun park with rides and games, a restaurant and a souvenir shop. A horse-riding trail from stables near Golden Bay passes by Anchor Bay. Other activities in the area include hiking, mountain biking, abseiling, jeep safaris, treasure hunts, beach games, water sports and carting.

---

**Popeye Village**
✉ Anchor Bay, Mellieħa.
☎ 21572430, 21570631.
📠 21570579.
info@popeyemalta.com
🕐 Apr–Sep: 10:00–18:00, Oct–Mar: closed.
💰 Adults: Lm3.30; children: Lm1.50.

---

**Below:** *Painted wooden houses at Popeye Village.*

While Malta's rocky foreshore is not ideal for serious hiking, there are good road walks along the coast. One from Valletta will take you past both Floriana and Marsamxett Harbour to Sliema and then St Julian's and St George's Bay. Another, from Marsascala, passes St Thomas Tower and St Thomas Bay, before crossing the Delimara peninsula to Marsaxlokk; from here you can walk on to Birżebbuġa.

**Below:** *Mdina Gate, the main entrance into the Silent City.*

## Walking Tours
### Valletta
A walk around the perimeter of Valletta on the road that follows its defensive curtain wall, yields unparalleled views across Marsamxett Harbour and Grand Harbour. It is a couple of hours well spent and there are open-air bars for refreshment on the way. The trip can also be done by traditional horse-drawn *karrozzin* – the views are just as good and you may be treated to an informative commentary.

### Mdina: A Stroll in the Silent City
At only 4ha (10 acres), Mdina is a city to wander in. Nowhere else can so much rich history be packed into so small an area – palaces, a cathedral, churches, museums, a convent, small piazzas and houses of the Maltese aristocracy are squeezed together inside the sturdy fortified walls and further protected by an enclosing dry moat.

There are three ways into the city – through **Mdina Gate**, past the horse-drawn *karrozzini* standing for hire on the Rabat side of the bridge; via **Greeks' Gate** leading from the moat at the far end of Howard Gardens; and through a hole in the wall on the west side. The latter was cut early this century to give Mdina's citizens a short cut to the new railway station below the walls; the railway, alas, no longer exists.

The ornamental Baroque archway of the Mdina Gate took its present form under Grand Master Manoel de Vilhena in 1724. The original access was at night across the drawbridge. At the same time the Greek's Gate, taking its name from the small Greek community who lived in the area, was similarly enhanced.

Mdina's main thoroughfare, **Villegaignon Street**, was named after the French knight Nicolas Durand de Villegaignon (1510–71), who founded Rio de Janeiro. It cuts from Mdina Gate to the high ramparts on the north side and is lined by most of the city's finest houses. To left and right as you amble through the quiet city are narrow streets and gently curving alleyways, so designed to protect the inhabitants from attack and the buildings from the strong summer sun.

**Above:** *Ornate design high above Villegaignon Street in Mdina.*

The street opens out into **St Paul's Square** before the great cathedral. Found at the far end of Villegaignon Street, behind the bulwark, is bougainvillea-flanked **Bastion Square**, with superb views across the Maltese landscape to St Paul's Bay, Grand Harbour and, in the middle distance, Mosta Dome and the National Stadium at Ta' Qali.

Entering through **Mdina Gate**, immediately on the right is the **Palazzo Vilhena**. It began life as the Magisterial Palace and was the inspiration of Maltese architect Giovanni Barbara in 1733. In 1909 it became the Connaught Hospital of the British and is now the **Museum of Natural History**.

**Horse-Drawn Cabs**
If the promenade walk from Sliema to St Julian's looks too taxing under the powerful sun, hail a *karrozzin*, Malta's traditional horse-drawn carriage, and travel there in style. There are *karrozzini* ranks at Sliema, St Julian's, Valletta and outside the gateway to Mdina.

**Above:** *From flowering fields in the centre of Malta rises the unmistakable shape of the city of Mdina.*

To the left, the reassuring blue lamp of Mdina police station hangs from the 16th-century **Tower of the Standard**. Its function has always been to protect the populace – originally fires were lit aloft to warn the citizens of an impending invasion. Directly ahead across **St Publius Square** is **St Peter's Monastery**, home of the Benedictine nuns, rebuilt in 1625 but 200 years older. The nuns are of a strict order that decrees they must be buried within the precincts; the only men allowed inside are the doctor, decorator, lawyer and undertaker – and then only with the bishop's permission.

Opposite the nunnery, at No. 3 Villegaignon Street, is imposing **Casa Inguanez**, the home since 1350 of Mdina's oldest family and once the hereditary governors of the city. The oldest house in Mdina – and reputedly in Malta – is **Palazzo Santa Sophia**, found on the left hand side of Villegaignon Street just past the cathedral near Holy Cross Street.

The large church on the left is the **Carmelite Church** and priory. Villegaignon Street opens on to **Bastion Square**; to your right, tucked inside the northern wall, is the **Fontanella tea garden**, one of few eating places in Mdina and certainly the most spectacularly situated. The tea and cakes are good, too.

## Organized Tours
### Valletta

Many local tour companies offer excursions from the main resort areas to Valletta. A typical tour takes in the Barracca Gardens, St John's Co-Cathedral, the National War Museum, Lascaris War Rooms and Palace of the Grand Masters. Sunday morning tours visit the market. Times and departure points vary. Contact **Josephine's**, ⊠ *80 The Strand, Sliema*, ☎ *21310435,* or **Nova Travel Services**, ⊠ *Bay Square, Buġibba,* ☎ *21575240.*

### Sliema and St. Julian's

**Island Tours** can be booked at Josephine's. **Boat trips** operate from the Strand at Sliema with **Captain Morgan Cruises**, ⊠ *Dolphin Court, Tigne Seafront, Sliema,* ☎ *21343373 or 21331961,* ☖ *21332004,* ✆ *info@captainmorgan.com.mt* ⌨ *www. captainmorgan.com.mt*

### The Three Cities

Half-day **coach tours** from Sliema and Buġibba take in the Three Cities, allowing time to visit the Maritime Museum and Inquisitor's Palace in Vittoriosa, the Cotonera Lines fortifications around Cospicua and Gardjola Garden overlooking Grand Harbour in Senglea. Operators include Josephine's and Nova Travel Services (details above). A two-hour excursion in a 1920s-style **vintage bus** runs twice daily from the Strand at Sliema to the Three Cities, operated by Captain Morgan Cruises – an authentic history lesson as the story of the Knights is recounted on board.

> #### Underwater Safaris
> If you fancy exploring the deep without getting your hair wet, the Underwater Safari boat of the **Captain Morgan** company operates several cruises daily from the small quay at Buġibba. A sophisticated improvement on the glass-bottomed boat, the Underwater Safari craft accommodates passengers in a glass-sided lounge below deck that affords excellent views of marine life through the crystal clear water.

**Below:** *A boat cruise explores Dockyard Creek.*

### Boat trips

Malta's excursion *par excellence* is the 75-minute **Harbour Cruise** that operates several times daily from the Strand at Sliema. The trip, with commentary, is a history lesson in itself. It lasts around an hour and a quarter and takes in every creek in Grand Harbour and Marsamxett Harbour. Other pleasure boats leave here for a day trip to **Comino** and an excursion around the islands; there are summer voyages on a three-masted schooner.

Boat trips also operate around the islands and to Comino's spectacular **Blue Lagoon**, where even the most committed landlubber will be tempted to take a dip. Other fascinating trips explore the subterranean world by glass-panelled underwater safari boat and submarine.

**Below:** *Old yellow buses link Valletta with every town and village.*

## The South

**Coach tours** from Sliema and Buġibba take in Malta's south, visiting Wied-iż-Żurrieq for boat trips to Blue Grotto and Marsaxlokk. The trips usually take in Marsascala and Birżebbuġa and visit the stone quarries near Mqabba. Longer excursions visit the temple sites at Tarxien and the Għar Dalam cave. Operators include Josephine's and Nova Travel Services (*see* page 47).

## Mdina and Rabat

**Coach tours** run from Sliema and Buġibba to Mdina and Rabat. Tours include a walk through Mdina, a visit to the cathedral and Cathedral Museum and a walk along the ramparts. Most tours also take in St Paul's and St Agatha'a Catacombs, the Grotto of St Paul, and the Roman Villa and Museum in Rabat. Operators include Josephine's and Nova Travel Services. Attractions presenting Mdina's colourful history are the **Mdina Dungeons** ✉ *St Publius Square,* ☎ *21450267;* the **Mdina Experience** ✉ *Mesquita Square,* ☎ *21454322;* **Medieval Times** ✉ *Palazzo Notabile,* ☎ *21454625;* **Tales of the Silent City** ✉ *Villegaignon Street,* ☎ *21451179;* and **Knights of Malta** ✉ *Magazine Street,* ☎ *21451342.*

## The Centre

Half-day and full-day **coach tours** operate from Malta's principal resort areas to attractions in the centre of the island. Among sites visited are the Ta' Qali Craft Centre, the

Dinosaurs Exhibition and the Mosta Dome. Tours also visit San Anton Gardens and Buskett Gardens. Excursion operators to the centre of the island are Josephine's and Nova Travel Services (*see page 47*). A five-hour **Vintage Village excursion** to Naxxar includes a bus tour operated by Captain Morgan Cruises (*see page 47*).

## The North

Captain Morgan Cruises operates **boat trips** from Buġibba to Comino and around Gozo; they also have an **Underwater Safari boat**.

## Gozo

Full-day **excursions** operate to Gozo from the resorts on Malta. **Jeep safaris** go off the beaten track to parts of the island not seen on regular coach tours. **Evening trips** to Gozo take in the sunset at Dwejra. Principal operators include Josephine's and Nova Travel Services. **Boat trips** from Sliema and Buġibba visit Comino: Captain Morgan is the chief operator.

**Above:** *Excursion boats alongside St Paul's Bay jetty at Buġibba. Trips take in the bays of northern Malta and Comino.*

### Floating Taxis
The traditional way to cross Grand Harbour is by *dgħajsa* (pronounced 'dicer') – Malta's answer to the gondola – the high-prowed, brightly painted water taxi that once ferried Royal Navy sailors back to their ships. Traditionally propelled by a standing oarsman, they now have outboard motors. Many boats are based along Senglea's waterfront, so it may be easier to start a round-trip on the Three Cities side. Annual dgħajsa races are held in Grand Harbour on 8 September.

**Above:** *A small store in Valletta. Such family businesses are still common.*

## Shops

Sliema and St George's Bay are the places for international-style shopping at reasonable prices. There are shopping centres with music, fashions, perfumeries, shoes and brand names together with fast-food outlets, restaurants and cafés. In Sliema, shopping action is found on two main streets, Bisazza Street and Tower Road, but the side streets house interesting options, especially for fashion, sports, interiors and shoes. Up the coast, St George's Bay has excellent shopping, leisure and entertainment outlets.

Valletta has several shopping malls and arcades. Among the grid of streets with tiny craft shops, restorers and household shops, Valletta has designer names, fashion, music and much more.

### The Maltese Falcon, Mdina

If one takes a stroll through Villegaignon Street, Mdina's main street, you will find The Maltese Falcon opposite the Carmelite Church. It has a wide range of souvenirs such as blown glass, handmade silver and gold filigree, replicas of old swords and guns, books and videos on Maltese history in different languages, a selection of Maltese handmade lace, typical solid brass door knockers, post-cards and a selection of Maltese Falcons.

✉ *27 Villegaignon Street, Mdina,*
☎ *21456009,*
📠 *21459548,* 🖰 *info@ themaltesefalcon.com*
🖥 *www. themaltesefalcon.com*

## Home & Gift Centre, Attard

One of the largest of its kind in Malta, dedicated to quality household goods and giftware. Ample parking space; deliver anywhere in Malta. Major credit cards accepted.
✉ *M4 Shopping Complex, Old Railway Road, Attard,*
☎ */ 📠 21436285,*
🖰 *homeandgift@ europe.com*
🖥 *http://homeandgift. tripod.com*

## Cittadella Boutique, Victoria

The street to the left of Victoria's Cathedral leads to this one-stop shop for high-quality local lacework and food items.
✉ *4 Fosse Street, Victoria, Gozo,*
☎ *21555953,*
🕒 *Closed on Sundays.*

## Number 18, Buġibba

A souvenir and gift shop on the Buġibba seafront, where you can find many examples of local craftsmanship like Malta glass ornaments, china, pottery and a vast range of handmade wallhanging plates depicting local scenery.
✉ *18 Islets Promenade, Buġibba,*
☎ *21576520 or 99442919.*

## Eaton Jewellery, Buġibba

Gold and silver items, filigree, Maltese filigree crosses, watches, souvenirs and gifts.
✉ *Rock Cod Street, Buġibba,* ☎ *21581426.*

## Mdina Glass, Mdina

In the centre of the island, you can see glassblowers at work. *See panel, page 52.*
✉ *Ta 'Qali Craft Village,* ☎ *21415786,*
📠 *21415787,*
🕒 *Sat: 09:00–13:00; Mon–Fri: 08:00-16:30,*
🖰 *info@mdinaglass.net*
🖥 *www.mdinaglass.net*

*See panel, page 52.*

**Below:** *Fishermen unload their catch for the market at Marsaxlokk.*

## Markets

There are a number of interesting markets in Malta. For treasure hunting, search the bric-a-brac at **Il-Monti**, an open-air Sunday market just outside Valletta's city gate near the bus station. For more mainstream goods, try the daily market at Merchants Street, by St John's Square, Valletta, open Mon–Sat until noon. Other markets include a Tuesday morning market held on the outskirts of **Cospicua** and a daily morning market in **Rabat**.

## The Main Square (It-Tokk), Victoria

While the Citadel on its bluff first catches the eye, the real heart of Victoria in Gozo is its main square, **Pjazza Independenza** – better known by its old name of **It-Tokk**, meaning 'meeting place'. The small, tree-lined square at the top of Republic Street is fringed with tiny shops and bars and has a daily morning market selling fruit, vegetables and local craftware.

✉ *Independence Square, Victoria,* ☎ *21563344,* 📠 *21563355,* 🖱 *victoria.lc@magnet.mt* 🕐 *Sunday mornings.*

## Marsaxlokk Sunday Market

Marsaxlokk overlooks a bay packed in summer with traditional high-prowed *luzzu* fishing boats. Along the quay-side, the Sunday morn-ing market, selling everything from locally made lace tablecloths to freshly caught octopus, awakens the neighbours early and throughout the day attracts a succession of coach parties.

## Craft Centres
### Ta' Qali

Situated on the former World War II airfield, this is Malta's largest craft market. Craftsmen can be seen at work and their silver filigree jewellery, coloured Mdina glassware, ceramics, wicker furniture, wrought ironwork and items of Malta stone are all produced on site and well displayed. Prices are generally lower than in souvenir shops.

⊠ Off the Valletta-Rabat Road, ☎ 21415786, ⏰ 08:00–16:00, Mon–Fri.

### Ta' Dbiegi Crafts Village, Gozo

A variety of crafts are produced and sold here in Gozo.

⊠ San Lawrenz, Gozo, ☎ 21561974, ⏰ Winter 08:00–16:45, summer 08:30–18:45.

### Malta Crafts Centre, Valletta

This centre acts as a showcase of the Islands' crafts and provides more information on crafts and the best places to buy various items.

⊠ St John's Square (opposite the cathedral), Valletta. ⏰ Mid June to end of Sep: Mon–Fri, 09:00–12:30; Oct–mid June: Mon–Fri, 09:00–12:30 and 15:00–17:00.

### Empire Arts and Crafts Centre, Rabat

Rabat centre is good for handmade crafts; you can also watch lace, glass and silver filigree being made.

⊠ 20A/B St Agatha Street, Rabat, ☎ 21453245, 📠 21451095, ⏰ 09:00–17:00. 🖥 enquiries@empiremalta.com 💻 www.empiremalta.com

**Above:** *Colourful Maltese craftware for sale in the market place.*

---

**Shopping Spree**

Most Maltese shops are small, family-run businesses which have changed little over the decades. Maltese shoppers head for **Republic Street** in Valletta or for Sliema, while Valletta's **Sunday morning market** below St James Bastion, is one of Malta's top tourist attractions – and popular with the locals, too. Pick your way around stalls selling books, music tapes, clothes, household items – you name it and it's there. Along the edge of the market are many stalls with bric-a-brac and second-hand goods.

**Above:** *Water's-edge sunbathing patio and pool of the Fortina Hotel in Sliema.*

**Gozo's Farmhouses**
If you want luxurious accommodation off the beaten track, Gozo has the answer in its converted farmhouses. No expense has been spared in upgrading these rustic rural dwellings into superb and spacious holiday villas, often with their own swimming pool, courtyard and often a walled garden and rooftop terrace. This is upmarket tourism – you may even find a jacuzzi in your little corner of Gozo.

## WHERE TO STAY

Malta has hotels and self-catering properties to suit every pocket, from deluxe hotels to no-frills guesthouses, and luxury villas or converted farmhouses to basic apartments.

Hotels are graded from one to five stars and tourist villages and guesthouses from first to third class. Aparthotels, offering apartment-style accommodation with full hotel facilities, range from first to fourth class. The grading reflects both facilities and price. With few exceptions, tour operators feature hotels of three stars and above. Independent travellers should try to make their peak season reservations before arriving on the islands, as hotels fill up quickly. Gozo's converted self-catering farmhouses, often with their own pool, are luxurious. There are no official camping or caravan sites in the islands.

The Maltese government is trying to establish Gozo as an upmarket holiday spot and is encouraging the development of top-quality hotels such as L'Imġarr and the Kempinski San Lawrenz Resort & Spa (*see page 59*). The government is aware, however, that over-development could easily destroy Gozo's appeal and is now restricting the building of new holiday accommodation to deluxe standard. In keeping with this upmarket image, there are converted farmhouses and modern apartments.

## Valletta

### • *LUXURY*
**Le Meridien Phoenicia** (Map H–B2)
Grand old lady of Malta's hotels, built in 1947. Real five-star sophistication.
✉ The Mall, Floriana,
☎ 21225241,
📠 21235254, ⌂ info@phoenicia.com.mt
💻 www.lemeridienphoenicia.com

### • *MID-RANGE*
**Castille** (Map H–C2)
Central, near Upper Barracca Gardens; modest three-star with own wine bar.
✉ Castille Square, 348 St Paul Street,
☎ 21243677,
📠 21243679.

**Osborne** (Map H–C2)
Classy three-star in a quiet area of Valletta.
✉ 50 South Street,
☎ 21232127/8,
📠 21247293,
⌂ osbornehotel@vol.net.mt

### • *BUDGET*
**British** (Map H–C2)
Run by the same family since 1932, it belies its two-star rating.
✉ 40 Battery Street,
☎ 21224730,
📠 21239711, ⌂ info@britishhotel.com
💻 www.britishhotel.com

## Sliema

### • *LUXURY*
**Crowne Plaza** (Map G–D3)
Attractive five-star in quieter part of Sliema.
✉ Tigne Street,
☎ 21341173/83,
📠 21311292,
⌂ comments@crowneplazamalta.com
💻 http://malta.crowneplaza.com

### • *MID-RANGE*
**Best Western Les Lapins** (Map H–A2)
Marina-side four-star.
✉ Ta' Xbiex Yacht Marina, ☎ 21342551/8,
📠 21343902,
⌂ info@les-lapins.com
💻 www.les-lapins.com

**Fortina** (Map G–D3)
Malta's first all-inclusive hotel; four stars.
✉ Tigne Seafront,
☎ 21343380,
📠 21339388, ⌂ info@hotelfortina.com 💻
www.hotelfortina.com

**Howard Johnson Diplomat** (Map G–C2)
Four-star hotel.
✉ Tower Road,
☎ 21345361/6,
📠 21345351,
⌂ diplomat@vol.net.mt
💻 www.diplomat.com.mt

**Park** (Map G–D2)
Four-star property near the Preluna.
✉ Graham Street,
☎ 21343780,
📠 21343770, ⌂ info@parkhotel.com.mt
💻 www.parkhotel.com.mt

**Plevna** (Map G–D3)
Three-star in quiet area close to the sea.
✉ 2 Thornton Street, Sliema, ☎ 21331031,
📠 21336496,
⌂ roosendaal@waldonet.net.mt
💻 www.roosendaal.com.mt

**Preluna Hotel & Towers** (Map G–D2)
Four stars; high-rise seafront hotel.
✉ 124 Tower Road,

☎ 21334001/9,
📠 21337281, 🖅 info@
preluna-hotel.com
🖥 www.
preluna-hotel.com

## Waterfront
(Map G–B3)
Four-star overlooking
Marsamxett Harbour.
✉ The Strand, Gzira,
☎ 21333434,
📠 21333535,
🖅 info@water.mizzi.
com.mt 🖥 www.
waterfrontmalta.com

### • BUDGET
## Sliema Chalet
(Map G–D3)
Well-sited three-star
on Sliema's fashion-
able seafront road.
✉ 117 Tower Road,
☎ 21335575,
📠 21333249,
🖅 info@sliemachalet.
com 🖥 www.
sliemachalet.com

# St Julian's/
# Paceville
### • LUXURY
## Golden Tulip
## Vivaldi (Map G–A1)
Four-star in the heart
of the night-life area.
✉ Dragonara Road,
☎ 21378100,

📠 21378101,
🖅 sales@gtvivaldi.
goldentulip.nl
🖥 www.
goldentuliphotels.nl/
gtvivaldi

## Westin Dragonara
## Resort (Map G–B1)
Elegant five-star that's
better than most.
✉ Dragonara Road,
☎ 21381000,
📠 21378877,
🖅 westin.dragonara@
westin.com 🖥 www.
westinmalta.com

### • MID-RANGE
## Lapsi (Map G–B2)
Interesting modern
four-star just off the
seafront.
✉ Balluta Bay, St
Julian's, ☎ 21378800,
📠 21373227, 🖅 sales@
lapsihotels.com.mt
🖥 www.lapsihotels.
com.mt

### • BUDGET
## Miramare (Map G–B2)
Three-star occupying
a good seafront
location.
✉ Main Street, Balluta
Bay, St Julian's, ☎
21341160,
📠 21341838,

🖅 miramare@
robertarrigo.net

# St George's
# Bay
### • LUXURY
## Corinthia San Ġorġ
(Map D–F2)
New hotel offers five-
star luxury by the sea.
✉ St George's Bay,
☎ 21374114,
📠 21374039, 🖅
sangorg@corinthia.com
🖥 www.
corinthiahotels.com

## Radisson SAS Bay
## Point Resort
(Map D–F2)
Five-star by the sea.
☎ 374894, 📠 374895,
🖅 info@radisson.
com.mt 🖥 www.
islandhotels.com/
radisson

### • MID-RANGE
## Bernard (Map G–A1)
Across the street from
Bay Street mall and
handy for nightlife.
✉ St George's Bay, St
Julian's, ☎ 21373900,
📠 21314726,
🖅 hotelbernard@
hotelbernard.com.mt
🖥 www.
hotelsmalta.com

## The Three Cities

There are no hotels, holiday apartments, guesthouses or similar in Vittoriosa, Senglea and Cospicua. Good news is that you are only 20-minutes' drive from Sliema, where there is a wide range of accommodation.

## The South

• *LUXURY*

**Corinthia Jerma Palace** (Map D–H4)
Biggest and best in the south; distinctive four-star situated next to the sea on the edge of Marsascala.
⊠ *Dawret it-Torri, Marsascala,*
☎ *21633222,*
✆ *21639485,* ✆
*jerma@corinthia.com*
🖥 *www. corinthiahotels.com*

• *BUDGET*

**Etvan** (Map D–H4)
Three-star near the centre of Marsascala.
⊠ *Bahhara Street,*
☎ *21632323,*
✆ *21634330,*
✆ *info@etvan.com*
🖥 *www.etvan.com*

## Mdina and Rabat

• *LUXURY*

**Xara Palace**
(Map E–C2)
Palatial hotel in the 'silent city' of Mdina.
⊠ *Mdina,*
☎ *21450560,*
✆ *21452612,* ✆ *info@ xarapalace.com.mt*
🖥 *www. xarapalace.com.mt*

## The Centre

Malta's central region has only two hotels – the former Grand Hotel Verdala at Rabat, being rebuilt, and the Corinthia Palace. There are no holiday apartments or guesthouses in the area. Plenty of hotel and self-catering accommodation can be found by the coast in the Sliema/St Julian's area and in the St Paul's Bay resorts.

• *LUXURY*

**Corinthia Palace**
(Map D–E4)
Five-star elegance in one of Malta's few inland hotels, situated by San Anton Gardens.

Opened by the Duke of Edinburgh in 1968, it contains a health spa.
⊠ *De Paule Avenue, Balzan* ☎ *21440301/9,*
✆ *21465713,* ✆
*palace@corinthia.com*
🖥 *www. corinthiahotels.com*

## Qawra/St Paul's Bay

• *LUXURY*

**Grand Hotel Mercure Costa San Antonio** (Map C–D2)
Stylish four-star rebuild of the former Hyperion on the edge of Buġibba.
⊠ *St Paul's Bay,*
☎ *21572482,*
✆ *21572481,* ✆ *info@ costasanantonio.com*

**Suncrest** (Map C–E2)
Big and brash, it dominates Qawra's seafront with its water-side lido. At the very top of the four-star band.
⊠ *Qawra Coast Road,*
☎ *21577101,* ✆
*21575478,* ✆ *info@ suncresthotel.com*
🖥 *www. suncresthotel.com*

### • *MID-RANGE*

**Coastline** (Map C–F3)
Four-star; views across Salina Bay to Qawra.
☒ Salina Bay, Salina,
☎ 21573781,
℡ 21581104, ⌁
info@coastline.com.mt
⌨ www.
islandhotels.com

### Corinthia Mistra Village Clubhotel

(Map D–C2)
Best holiday complex in the islands; apart-ments around pool.
☒ Xemxija Hill,
☎ 21580481,
℡ 21582941, ⌁
mistra@corinthia.com
⌨ www.
corinthiahotels.com

### New Dolmen

(Map C–D2)
Modern four-star built around Neolithic re-mains at the meeting of Buġibba and Qawra.
☒ St Paul's Bay,
☎ 21581510/8,
℡ 21581081, ⌁ sales@
dolmen.com.mt ⌨
www.dolmen.com.mt

### Qawra Palace

(Map C–E2)
Good sea-facing location for the Suncrest's four-star neighbour; attractive seafront patio.
☒ Qawra Coast Road,
☎ 21580131,
℡ 21580662.

### • *BUDGET*

**Buġibba Holiday Complex** (Map C–D3)
Well-priced aparthotel complex in the St Paul's Bay resort area.
☒ Triq it Turisti, St Paul's Bay,
☎ 21580861,
℡ 21580867, ⌁
info@bhc.com.mt ⌨
www.islandhotels.com

**Concorde** (Map C–D3)
A three-star in the heart of Buġibba.
☒ Pioneer Road, Buġibba, ☎ 21573831,
℡ 21573292, ⌁
admin@roosendaal.
com.mt ⌨ www.
roosendaal.com.mt

## Mellieħa area

### • *LUXURY*

**Grand Hotel Mercure Selmun Palace** (Map D–C2)
Hilltop location for this four-star; popular with continental visitors.
☒ Selmun,
☎ 21521040, ℡
21521060, ⌁ h2028@
accor-hotels.com

### • *MID-RANGE*

**Mellieħa Bay**
(Map D–B2)
Four-star favoured by the British, with splen-did views across the bay and beach to Mellieħa village.
☒ Ghadira,
☎ 21573844/5,
℡ 21576399, ⌁ info@
melliehabayhotel.com
⌨ www.
melliehabayhotel.com

## Bays to the north

### • *MID-RANGE*

**New Paradise Bay**
(Map D–A2)
Large four-star next to Gozo ferry terminal.
☒ Ċirkewwa
☎ 21573981,
℡ 21573115, ⌁
paradise@global.net.mt
⌨ www.
paradise-bay.com

### Ramla Bay

(Map D–B1)
Remote four-star at the end of a lane off Marfa Ridge facing Comino.

✉ Marfa, Ċirkewwa,
☎ 21522181,
✆ 21575391,
✆ ramlabay@
digigate.net
💻 www.digigate.net/
ramlabay

## Northern Gozo

### • LUXURY

**Cornucopia** (Map B–B2) Superb four-star farmhouse at Xagħra with great pool area.
✉ 10 Ġnien Imrik Street, Xagħra,
☎ 21556486,
✆ 21552910,
✆ cornucopia@
vjborg.com
💻 www.vjborg.com

### • MID-RANGE

**Calypso** (Map B–B1) No-frills three-star hotel on the quayside.
✉ Marsalforn Bay, Gozo, ☎ 21562000,
✆ 21562012,
✆ hotelcalypso@
gozo.com

## Southern Gozo

### • LUXURY

**Ta' Ċenċ** (Map B–B3) Outstanding five-star hotel, bungalow-style

rooms, in extensive grounds near Sannat.
✉ 1 Ta' Ċenċ Street, Sannat, ☎ 21561522,
✆ 21558199, ✆
tacenc@vjborg.com
💻 www.vjborg.com

### • MID-RANGE

**St Patrick's** (Map B–B3) Comfortable four-star hotel at water's edge.
✉ 12 Xlendi Seafront,
☎ 21562951,
✆ 21556598,
✆ st.patricks@
vjborg.com
💻 www.vjborg.com

## Eastern Gozo

### • LUXURY

**L'Imġarr** (Map B–C2) Five-star clifftop hotel above Mġarr harbour with spectacular views of Comino and Malta.
✉ Mġarr, Gozo
☎ 21560455,
✆ 21557589, ✆ info@
mgarrhotel.com
💻 www.vol.net.mt/
mgarr/imgarr1.htm

### • MID-RANGE

**Grand** (Map B–C2) New four-star above Mġarr harbour – handy for the ferries.

✉ St Anthony Street, Għajnsielem, Gozo,
☎ 21563840,
✆ 21559744,
✆ reservations@
grandhotelmalta.com
💻 www.
grandhotelmalta.com

## Western Gozo

### • LUXURY

**Kempinski San Lawrenz Resort & Spa** (Map B–A2) Modern five-star resort offering real seclusion in the heart of the Gozo countryside.
✉ San Lawrenz, Gozo,
☎ 21558640,
✆ 21562977, ✆
info@sanlawrenz.com
💻 www.
sanlawrenz.com

## Comino

### • MID-RANGE

**Comino** (Map D–A1) Hotel and bungalows in adjacent bays provide the only accommodation on tiny Comino.
☎ 21529821,
✆ 21529826, ✆ info@
cominohotels.com
💻 www.
cominohotels.com

**Vegetable Dishes**
Malta has a number of vegetable-based dishes using local produce. Among the more popular are *ful bit-tewm* (broad beans with garlic), *qacoq mimli* (globe artichokes stuffed with anchovy, olives, garlic and parsley), *bzar ahdar mimli* (stuffed green peppers), *zebbug mimli* (stuffed olives), *kabocci* (cabbage, boiled and then fried with bacon) and *pastard bil gbejniet* (cauliflower, boiled and then fried with goat's cheese).

## EATING OUT
## What to Eat

Consider the many foreign influences that have shaped Malta's character and it follows that the country's cuisine will be broad based – vaguely **Mediterranean**, flavoured with Italian and a dash of the British; with a hint of Arabian. Many restaurants steer a culinary course between **British** and **Italian**, to satisfy the conservative palates of holiday-makers.

While genuine Maltese dishes appear on some menus, there are still few restaurants specializing in the traditional cuisine of the islands. Nevertheless, many provide excellent fare, often in a rustic Maltese setting – though it is not necessarily the best for those thinking about their diet. Don't be put off by the sun-faded pictures of food outside.

### Fruit and Vegetables

**Below:** *Colourful Spinola Bay at St Julian's is home to a number of popular restaurants.*

Locally grown **vegetables** such as green peppers, globe artichokes, cabbage, cauliflower, aubergines and marrows play a big part in Maltese cuisine. They can be stuffed

with anchovies, minced pork or cheese to make a filling meal, possibly accompanied by thick chunks of Malta's excellent crusty **bread**.

Dried as well as fresh beans are yet another mainstay. Look out for *bigilla*, a thick pâté of broad beans with garlic. Another vegetable speciality is *kapunata*, a Maltese version of ratatouille made from tomatoes, capers, aubergines and green peppers.

**Above:** *A selection of home-grown Maltese fare.*

Fresh **fruits** available on the Maltese islands include oranges, figs, plums, peaches, grapes and melons.

## Soup

There are a variety of traditional soups – *minestra* is a heavy soup with pasta and vegetables; *aljotta* is boiled fish soup with tomatoes and garlic; and *kusksu* is a hearty soup made of fresh broad beans. *Soppa tal-armla* (widow's soup) is a filling soup with *gbejniet* (sheep or goat's cheese), ricotta cheese, eggs, lettuce, peas, carrots and onions.

## Meat Dishes

A favourite dish in Malta is *fenek* – rabbit, simmered country-style in wine, baked or in a stew. Another popular dish is *braġoli* (beef olives), which consist of thin slices of beef rolled around a mixture of minced ham and pork, bacon, egg and peas. *Ross il-Forn* is a baked rice dish with minced pork and beef, bacon, eggs and ricotta cheese.

---

**Maltese Bread**
Malta's excellent crusty bread has its origins with the bakeries established by the Knights. Their recipes exist today with few modifications – the flat *ftira* bread is still popular while larger loaves have a thick crust and nutty flavour. **Qormi** is reputed to produce the best bread and at one time was known as the village of the bakers; in some towns and villages you can buy bread still hot from a wood-burning oven.

## Pasta Dishes

*Ravjul* (ravioli) consists of familiar pasta shapes filled with ricotta cheese rather than meat; and *timpana* is a golden brown baked macaroni dish with minced beef and pork, eggs, cheese, chicken liver and bacon.

## Seafood

The Maltese serve fish in many ways – fried, grilled, poached, baked and stuffed, stewed, in a pie and with a variety of tasty sauces. Many restaurants offer a 'fresh fish of the day' – you might see *pixxispad* (swordfish), *acciola* (amberjack), *dentici* (sea bream), *cerna* (grouper), *tunnagg* (tuna), *merluzzo* (red mullet), *dott* (stone bass) and *fanfru* (pilot fish) – plus a Maltese speciality, the *lampuka*, which breeds in the Nile delta and is in season from early September until late November. In *torta tal-Lampuka* (lampuka pie) it is usually accompanied by onions, tomatoes, spinach, olives and capers in flaky pastry. Swordfish, octopus and squid are very often served in a sauce made of onions, tomatoes, olives and capers. Lobster and prawns are also available.

## Desserts and Pastries

That the Maltese have a **sweet tooth** is clear from the huge variety of cream-filled cakes and pastries on sale in kiosks and coffee shops. You cannot fail to notice the sweet aroma of frying *imqaret* (date slices with aniseed) or be surprised by the many varieties of *qubbajt* (nougat) at festa occasions. A favourite delicacy is *kannoli*, deep-fried crisp pastry stuffed with fresh ricotta and sweetened with pieces of chocolate and candied fruit. Other popular pastries are *helwa tat-Tork,* which consists of a sweet sugary mixture of crushed and whole almonds; and *pastizzi*, which are puff pastry cakes filled with ricotta cheese. The sweet specialities at Easter are the almond-flavoured iced biscuits called *figolli*.

## Snacks

A perfect snack is *hobz biz-zejt*, served in nearly every bar and still the 'packed lunch' of farmers and workmen. It is a large, thick round of bread dipped in olive oil, rubbed with ripe tomatoes and filled with a mixture of tuna, onion, garlic, tomatoes and capers. In restaurants smaller *bruschetta* are served as appetisers.

## Fast Food

Fast food and medium-fast food has long been an established way of dining in Malta. There are dozens of **pizzerias** in resort areas, and several international fast-food chains are now well represented in major centres.

> **Culinary Heritage**
>
> Maltese cuisine is the result of a long relationship between the islanders and the many foreigners who settled in Malta over the centuries. The influences are too numerous to list, but many popular Maltese specialities are Sicilian or Moorish in origin. As in all parts of the Mediterranean, the daily main meal, usually served at lunchtime, is an occasion to bring the family together. Due to a renewed interest in traditional Maltese food, many restaurants have been encouraged to offer some of this local fare.

**Below:** *Valletta's alfresco cafés are popular, especially in summer.*

# EATING OUT

## The Wine Industry

There are around 15 wineries in Malta and Gozo producing wine for the home market; some produce only a few thousand bottles annually and the larger ones turn out hundreds of thousands. The two leading wine manufacturers, Marsovin and Emmanuel Delecata, both offer wine tours with tastings. Contact:

**Marsovin,**
✉ The Winery, Marsa.
☎ 21824920. 📠
21809501. 🖂 cellars@marsovin.com.mt
🖥 www.marsovin.com

**Emmanuel Delicata,**
✉ The Winery, Paola.
☎ 21825199. 📠
21672623. 🖂 emmdel@waldonet.net.mt
🖥 www.delicata.com

---

## What to Drink

Through the introduction of a greater number of quality wines in recent years, Malta is now taken much more seriously by wine drinkers. Wines such as Cabernet Sauvignon, Chardonnay, Merlot, Pinot Bianco, Pinot Grigio and Sauvignon Blanc are now found on the supermarket shelves. With Maltese wines, you get what you pay for; wines at the top of the range are good while those lower down, while drinkable, can take some getting used to.

Grapes are usually imported from Sicily and the northern and southern regions of Italy, although some grapes are grown on the slopes around Mellieħa. Long hot summers mean Maltese grapes ripen earlier so you can taste this year's wines all the earlier. The main wineries organise guided tours and tastings. Depending on the season, tours cover the entire production from the initial fermentation through to the ageing process. They also include wine history museums and opportunities to taste and buy a variety of vintages.

More adventurous imbibers might try wine from Gozo – powerful stuff with a high alcohol content that has been known to induce a couple of hours' sleep. Local beers like **Cisk** (lager) and **Hopleaf** (pale ale) are good; so is the bittersweet **Kinnie**, a Maltese soft drink now being exported.

*Below: Some of the wines produced on Gozo.*

## Where to Eat

Finding a place to eat in Malta is seldom a problem. Eat cheaply or expensively according to your pocket, your mood and your taste – from a simple bowl of pasta in the sun to something far more formal with several courses that demands collar and tie.

Malta's resort areas of Sliema, St Paul's Bay and St Julian's have a high concentration of places to eat out and other restaurants and cafés are scattered throughout the islands. For the widest choice head for the St Julian's/Paceville area – here there are also a large number of discos and music bars (see Pubs and Clubs, page 77).

The capital Valletta has relatively few restaurants; a much wider choice is available in nearby Sliema. Besides the traditional Maltese restaurants, other options include Indian, Chinese, Greek, Italian and Turkish restaurants, as well as pizzerias and pasta-houses aplenty. You can also dine well in hotel restaurants, many of which serve a traditional Sunday lunch.

**Above:** *The cafés along the promenade at Xlendi, on Gozo, are ideal for relaxation and people-watching.*

<u>**Late Night Dining**</u>
If it's a late, late meal you want, head for St Julian's and St George's Bay. Outlets at the Corinthia San Ġorġ/Corinthia Marina hotels open until 01:00 or 02:00, are Café 24, Dine and Dukes and Henry J Beans. Others include All Stars at the Vivaldi Hotel, the Dragonara Casino Brasserie and Le Bistro at the Radisson SAS Bay Point Hotel (24 hours). In Gozo, the Café Jubilee in Victoria and Otters in Marsalforn are open until 01:00.

# Malta
## VALLETTA AND SURROUNDS
## Valletta
### • LUXURY
**The Carriage**

Good value; menu of the week is a highlight. ⊠ 22/5 Valletta Buildings, South Street, ☎ 21247828, ☏ 21223048.

**Giannini**

Daily specialities support more expensive Italian-style menu. ⊠ 23 Windmill Street, St Michael's Bastion, ☎ 21237121, ☏ 21236575.

### • MID-RANGE
**Bologna**

Popular, good-value lunchtime venue with wide Italian menu. ⊠ 59 Republic Street, ☎ 21246149, ☏ 21250126, ⊕ bolognarestaurant@ kemmunet.net.mt

**Malata**

Unusual specialities; changes daily. Good blackboard menu. ⊠ Palace Square, ☎ 21233967.

**Scalini**

Medium-priced steak, fish and pasta menu. ⊠ 32D South Street, ☎ 21246221.

**Trattoria Parolaccia**

French and Italian dishes amid paintings by local artists. ⊠ Archbishop Street, ☎ 21250169.

### • BUDGET
**British**

Moderately-priced Maltese selection. ⊠ St Ursula Street, ☎ 21224730.

**Caffè Cordina**

Traditional coffeehouse with vaulted, frescoed ceiling. ⊠ Republic Street.

**Sicilia**

Inexpensive, topquality lunchtime fish and pasta. ⊠ 1A St John Street, ☎ 21240569.

## Sliema
### • LUXURY
**Il-Galeone**

Good Italian restaurant with a range of house specialities. ⊠ Tigne Seafront, ☎ 21316420.

### • MID-RANGE
**T.G.I. Friday's**

American-themed restaurant in a 19thcentury British fort. ⊠ Tower Road, ☎ 21346897/8.

### • BUDGET
**Blondino**

Inexpensive and appetizing seafood. ⊠ 15 Ghar il-Lembi Street, ☎ 21344605.

**Pizza Place**

Among the best pizzas in town. ⊠ Crowne Plaza, ☎ 21341173/83.

## St Julian's
### • LUXURY
**Barracuda**

Higher-priced, quality, water's-edge dining. ⊠ 194 Main Street, ☎ 21331817, ☏ 21337370, ⊕ barracuda@ wgc-group.com

**L-Ghonnella,**

Top-quality dining on the terrace of the Spinola Palace.

✉ *Spinola Palace,*
☎ *21341027.*

### • MID-RANGE
### Fayrouz
Intimate Middle
Eastern restaurant.
✉ *Borg Olivier Street,*
☎ *21320837.*

### La Dolcé Vita
Lively fish restaurant.
✉ *Spinola Bay,*
☎ *21337036.*

### San Giuliano
Popular Italian in a
former boathouse.
✉ *3 St Joseph Street,*
*Spinola Bay,*
☎ *21332000.*

## Paceville
### • LUXURY
### Baruffa
Higher priced quality.
✉ *27 Ball Street,*
☎ *21342728.*

### • MID-RANGE
### Il Brigante
Excellent Maltese
specialities.
✉ *Ball Street,*
☎ *21311774.*

### • BUDGET
### Ir-Rokna
One of Malta's oldest
restaurants/pizzerias.
✉ *Church Street,*
☎ *21311556.*

## The Three Cities
There is very little
choice in the environs
of the Three Cities.
Two **kiosks** on
Senglea's promenade
will serve something-
and-chips, but that is
the nearest you'll get
to haute cuisine. The
kiosks stay open late;
they are worth at least
a drink, if only for the
view across Dockyard
Creek. There are a few
takeaway **pizzerias**,
otherwise small bars
might be able to rustle
up a sandwich.
For a **restaurant** meal,
head west to Sliema or
St Julian's, where the
choice is extensive.
Another option is
Marsascala, 15-min-
utes' drive east; here
too there is a selection
of good restaurants.

## THE EAST
## Marsaxlokk
### • LUXURY
### Hunters' Tower
More expensive
seafront restaurant;
good fish dishes; excel-
lent range of starters.
✉ *Wilga Street,*
*Marsaxlokk,*
☎ *21651792.*

### • MID-RANGE
### Is-Sajjied
Good anti-pasto selec-
tion and fresh fish.
✉ *Xatt is-Sajjieda,*
*Marsaxlokk,*
☎ *21682549.*

### Pisces
Modern style; splen-
did, inexpensive fish.
✉ *49/50 Xatt is-*
*Sajjieda, Marsaxlokk,*
☎ *21684956,*
✆ *piscesrestaurant@*
*mailcity.com*

## Marsascala
### • MID-RANGE
### L'Awwista
Mid-priced fish; over-
looking the bay.
✉ *8 Zonqor Road,*
*Marsascala,*
☎ *21632022.*

### Red Lobster
Fish menu (and
lobster, of course).
✉ *Triq Il-Qaliet,*
*Marsascala,*
☎ *21687322.*

## Sottovoce

Good value Mediterr-
anean menu includes
24 pasta dishes.
✉ 29 Marina
Promenade,
Marsascala,
☎ 21632669.

## St Thomas Bay
• *LUXURY*
**Langustini**

Quality fish restaurant
near St Thomas Bay.
✉ Triq Id-Dahla, Ta'
San Tumas,
☎ 21687590.

• *MID-RANGE*
**Fisherman's Rest**

Off the tourist track,
inexpensive and hard
to beat for seafood.
✉ St Thomas Bay,
☎ 21632049.

• *BUDGET*
**San Tomaso**

Alfresco dining in
summer; excellent
lunchtime pasta.
✉ St Thomas Bay,
☎ 21639394.

## CENTRE AND SOUTH

There aren't too many
restaurants in middle
Malta. The Corinthia
Palace Hotel and a few
places in Mdina are
the best bet, plus one
beyond Dingli. Do-it-
yourself picnickers
should try Qormi, vil-
lage of the bakers, for
a crusty loaf, perhaps
with local goat's
cheese and a bottle
of Maltese wine.

## Dingli
• *BUDGET*
**Bobbyland**

Reasonably priced
Maltese specialities
on Dingli cliffs.
✉ Panoramic Road,
Dingli, ☎ 21452895,
📞 21453930.

## Mdina

Mdina tends to cater
for those requiring
either a full four-
course blow-out or
just tea and cakes –
not much in between.

• *LUXURY*
**Bacchus**

Within Mdina's fortifi-
cations, a wide menu
in upper price range.
✉ 1 Inguanez Street,
Mdina, ☎ 21454981,
📞 21459437, ⟶
bacchus@maltanet.net

## Medina

Sophisticated dining
in the Silent City.
✉ 7 Holy Cross Street,
Mdina, ☎ 21454004,
📞 21450587, 🖥 www.
mol.net.mt/medina
⟶ medina@vel.net.mt

• *MID-RANGE*
**Palazzo Notabile**

Extensive Maltese
selection in a 17th-
century palace.
✉ Villegaignon
Street, Mdina,
☎ 21454625.

• *BUDGET*
**Ciappetti**

Tea gardens with views
from the bastions.
✉ St Agatha's
Esplanade, Mdina.

## Fontanella

Light meals atop the
bastions; tea and
cakes are a speciality.
✉ Bastion Street,
Mdina.

## Rabat

There are very few
restaurants in Rabat
but the **Cosmana
Navarra** offers snacks
in the courtyard oppo-
site St Paul's Church.

## NORTH AND WEST
## Mellieħa
### • LUXURY
### The Arches
More expensive, but with a reputation for top-class cuisine.
✉ 113 G Borg Olivier Street, Mellieħa,
☎ 21523460.

## Mistra Bay
### • MID-RANGE
### Palazzo Santa Rosa
Slightly more expensive, in a converted farmhouse by the sea. Excellent starters.
✉ Mistra Bay,
☎ 21582736.

## Qawra
### • LUXURY
### Savini
Grand dining, upper-range Italian cuisine with excellent service.
✉ Qawra Road, Qawra, ☎ 21576927,
☏ 21418315.

### • MID-RANGE
### It-Tokk
Traditional Maltese dishes served buffet-style in a rustic setting.
✉ Suncrest Hotel, Qawra,
☎ 21577101.

### • BUDGET
### Coral Reef
Moderate prices with good fish selection.
✉ Suncrest Hotel, Qawra, (see page 57),
☎ 21577101.

## St Paul's Bay
### • MID-RANGE
### Da Rosi
Fish restaurant, all-round menu.
✉ 44 Church Street, St Paul's Bay,
☎ 21571411.

### • BUDGET
### Gillieru
Inexpensive; good reputation for fish.
✉ 66 Church Street, St Paul's Bay seafront,
☎ 21573480,
☏ 21572318.

## Gozo
### GOZO
## Għarb
### • MID-RANGE
### Jeffreys
Splendid value, hand-written menu which changes daily; rural ambience. May be closed in winter.
✉ 10 Għarb Road, Għarb, ☎ 21561006,
☏ 21557246.

## Victoria
### • MID-RANGE
### Vineyard
Large medium-priced menu.
✉ Mġarr Road, Victoria, ☎ 21559976.

## Xagħra
### • MID-RANGE
### Cornucopia Hotel
Great lunchtime pasta, good evening selection.
✉ Gnien Imrik Street, Xagħra, ☎ 21556486,
☏ 21552910.

### Oleander
Great value, authentic Gozitan meals.
✉ 10 Victory Square, Xagħra, ☎ 21557230.

## Xlendi
### • MID-RANGE
### Kenur
Good mid-priced selection. Also has a fixed-price menu.
✉ Victoria Road, Xlendi, ☎ 21551583.

### St Patrick's
Good à la carte menu at reasonable prices by the sea.
✉ Xlendi Seafront,
☎ 21562951.

## ENTERTAINMENT
### Nightlife

Malta may not be renowned for its dynamic nightlife, but what there is caters adequately for a fairly wide cross-section of holiday-makers and includes a **theatre**, **casino**, **cinemas** and **discos**. Most hotels offer entertainment of some kind, such as sing-along **piano bar**, **cabaret** or colourful **folk-dancing**. The Islands have a vibrant calendar of theatre and concerts, classical and modern. Many are held outdoors or in historic venues. For a lively night out, nothing beats a summer festa. Saints, fireworks, food and fun are all part of this cultural phenomenon; one not to be missed.

### Music

Malta hosts several major music festivals as well as weekly musical events. There are organ recitals in Baroque churches and regular orchestral and soloist concerts in historic venues such as the Manoel Theatre and St James Cavalier. Annual music festivals include the Valletta Baroque Festival; the summer Arts Festival; the Opera Festival; the Choir Festival; and the Malta Jazz Festival. Jazz nights are often held at the Cavalier, and in several café-bars.

Ghana (pronounced 'aana') is Maltese folk music at its most individual and traditional. Ghana originated in village bars

**Opposite:** *The Porte des Bombes gateway into Floriana. Along with many of the suburb's fortifications, it is attractively floodlit at night.*
**Below:** *Msida's creek-side parish church of St Joseph all dressed up for the summer festa.*

and is always sung by men, accompanied by guitar. The lyrics tell stories of village life and of events in local history. You may experience an impromptu Ghana in a rural bar.

If it's loud music you're after, head for the neon-adorned music bars of Paceville and St George's Bay, thundering out their wild range of dance, house, rap and reggae offerings. There are some good hi-tech discos with wall-to-wall lasers and advanced sound systems to satisfy the most sophisticated boppers.

## Theatre

The **Manoel Theatre**, Malta's cultural hub, stages ballet, opera and concerts by its own symphony orchestra. Plays are performed, but rarely in English. Cultural gatherings have taken place in the theatre since 1731, when Grand Master Manoel de Vilhena ordered that it be built 'for the honest recreation of the people', with funding from his own pocket. The little box theatre is one of Europe's oldest and after years of neglect and misuse, has now regained its old glory.

## Film

Film buffs have been spoilt for choice since the expansion of the Eden Film Centre at St George's Bay to 16 screens, showing an interesting blend of brand new releases and older films – all in English. Other multi-screen cinema complexes have sprung up elsewhere on the island. Be prepared for incessant chatter and popcorn crunching during the film; also for the sudden picture fade-out and interval.

**Astra Theatre**
⊠ 9 Republic Street, Victoria. ☎ 21556256. ℂ 21559366.

**Aurora Theatre**
⊠ Republic Street, Victoria. ☎ 21562974.

**Bay Street Theatre**
⊠ St George's Bay, St Julian's.
☎ 2137922111. ℅ info@baystreet.com.mt

**Manoel Theatre**
⊠ 115 Old Theatre Street, Valletta. ☎ 21246389/21222618. ℂ 21247451. ▢ www.teatrumanoel.com.mt ℅ mtadmin@ teatrumanoel.com.mt ⊕ box office: Mon–Fri 10:00–12:00, 17:00–19:00; Sat 10:00–12:00. 🚌 Mon–Fri 10:30 and 11:30, Sat 11:30. No tours Sundays and public holidays. ⓓ Lm1.50.

**Republic Theatre**
⊠ Mediterranean Conference Centre, Valletta (see page 17). ☎ 21243840/6. ℅ info@mcc.com.mt

**Above:** *The Wartime Experience records the siege of 1940–43.*

## Mediterranean Film Studios

Close to Grand Harbour, for centuries the hub of Malta's seafaring activity, the modern Mediterranean Film Studios provide movie-makers with a unique sea setting. Two large circular water tanks, cleverly sited to show the sky as a backdrop, have been used in countless films and TV series – *Howards Way* and *Christopher Columbus* are examples. One tank is for surface filming and the other for shooting underwater scenes. The studios are close to Fort Ricasoli (see page 30).

## Shows

### The Wartime Experience

Malta's wartime history is recounted in a 45-minute sound and light show at the Discovery Centre in the Bay Street complex, St Julian's. Original film footage and still material are used in a vivid presentation of the war effort. The Wartime Experience has been re-recorded with new footage and better quality sound.

### The Malta Experience

This established and popular screen attraction brings history to life at the Mediterranean Conference Centre (see page 17), where Malta's fascinating story from Neolithic times to the present is told in an ever-changing kaleidoscope of images – 1100 colour slides from 21 projectors with sound effects, are accompanied by multi-lingual commentary.

---

**Mediterranean Film Studios**
✉ RL5, St Rocco Street, Kalkara.
☎ 21678151/2/3.
📠 21674434.
📧 info@mfsstudios.com
💻 www.mfsstudios.com

**The Wartime Experience**
✉ Embassy Cinema Complex, Sta Lucia Street, Valletta.
☎ 21227436.
📠 21227437.
🕐 Shows: 10:00–13:00 daily. 💰 Adults: Lm2; Children: Lm1.50.

**The Malta Experience**
✉ St Elmo Bastions, Mediterranean Street, Valletta. ☎ 21243776.
📠 21249426.
🕐 Shows: hourly 11:00–16:00, Mon–Fri; 11:00–13:00 weekends and public holidays.
📧 mxp@maltanet.net
💻 www.themaltaexperience.com/HomeA.htm

## Radio and Television

For such a small population, the Maltese people enjoy a vast selection of radio stations and TV channels – at the last count, 22 radio stations including local community stations; eight local TV stations, 10 Italian TV stations and around 40 available on cable/satellite. While TV Malta remains the country's prime TV station, the Italian channels are popular with Maltese viewers – the high-masted TV aerials seen around the island are needed for tuning in to Italy.

## Casinos

If you fancy a flutter, the **Dragonara Casino** grants free membership to visitors. Take up the offer – the inside is worth a look. The colonnaded square building standing well aloof from the buzz of Paceville and St George's Bay on Dragonara Point was formerly the elegant 19th-century summer villa of Marquis Scicluna and his noble Maltese family. It is reached through a gateway bearing the Latin inscription *Deus nobis haec otia fecit*, translating as 'God made this haven for us'. The gaming hall, with its roulette, black jack and *chemin de fer* tables, was once the Dragonara Palace courtyard, around which the interconnecting rooms of the villa were built. There is a slot-machine section and restaurant within the casino. (*See* side panel for more information on casinos.)

**Dragonara Casino**
✉ Dragonara Palace, St. Julian's.
☎ 21382362/4.
📠 21382371.
🖥 casino@dragonara.com
💻 www.dragonara.com
🕐 Mon–Thurs 10:00–06:00 and Fri–Sun 24 hours. Table games open at 11:00 Mon–Thurs and 24 hours Fri–Sun.

**Oracle Casino**
✉ St Paul's Promenade, Qawra.
☎ 21570057.
📠 21574118. 🖥
win@oraclecasino.com
💻 www.oraclecasino.com
🕐 The casino is open every day from 10:00.
🍽 Delphi Brasserie.

**Casino' di Venezia**
✉ Captain's Palace, The Waterfront, Vittoriosa.
☎ 21805580.
📠 21667591.
🖥 info@casinodivenezia.com.mt
🕐 11:00–04:00.

**Below:** *The Dragonara Casino, St George's Bay.*

**Below:** *A statue of the risen Christ is paraded through St Julian's on Easter Sunday.*

## Festivals

### The Village Festa

To the uninitiated, staccato crackling in the air above and accompanying bursts of thick smoke might imply that one Maltese village has declared war on another. To everyone else, the aerial explosions mean that another *festa* (festival) is under way. This is the highlight of every parish calendar, a five-day celebration of its patron saint's feast day wrapped round a weekend of non-stop action that successfully blends piousness with wild celebration. In the days preceeding the festa, fireworks explode in ever-increasing numbers above the village in a countdown to the big weekend – if you are in Malta in July or August you will be well aware of them. Highlight is the *giggi-fogu*, where fireworks mounted on poles in the village square are set off one at a time in a truly spectacular show.

The festa season kicks off on the third Sunday after Easter with the Feast of **St Publius** in Floriana, and continues through to **September**. The parish church is dressed, ornamented and lit up by hundreds of light bulbs for the occasion. The result is stunning – nowhere more than at **Msida**, where the lights on the parish church of St Joseph reflect vividly in Msida Creek. Then come the decorations – the statues of saints lining every street, the bunting draped from house to house, the flags atop every other building and

yet more fairy lights strung between poles. Inside, the saint's statue is adorned with flowers. After the services, crowds follow the statue through the streets. A brass band plays and there is general merrymaking late into the night, culminating in a spectacular firework display which the villagers have saved for all year. The festival displays are memorable and demonstrate strong rivalry between parishes each determined to put on bigger and better exhibitions than their neighbours.

After a period in the 1970s and 1980s when it was held in May, **Carnival** in Malta is now firmly established in the period immediately preceding Lent, to herald the approaching end of winter and arrival of spring. Carnival was started by the Knights in the 16th century, when it was led by the Grand Master; now towns and villages throughout Malta join in the celebrations with fancy-dress parades, lavishly decorated floats, folk dancing and, of course, firework displays. The biggest and most colourful procession takes place through the streets of Valletta.

**Above:** *Banners decorate the streets of towns and villages at festa time.*

**Maltese Christmas**
The Maltese enjoy celebrating Christmas – decorating their houses and streets elaborately for the festive season. Nativity scenes adorn many front windows; cress is traditionally planted around the base of a crib containing a porcelain baby Jesus. In the south of the island, illuminated orange folded paper stars are hung in upstairs bay windows, their light glowing against a back curtain. Streets and churches in the towns and villages are hung with coloured lights that include the Maltese 'shooting star' decoration; many parishes have their own crib scene.

**Above:** *Trotting meeting at the Marsa Race Track.*

### Trotting

Malta's menfolk (but very few women) turn out in force on Sunday afternoons for the trotting meetings at Marsa, to enjoy the programme of a dozen or so races that takes nearly five hours to complete. Bet on the Tote (minimum 50c forecast; Lm1 win or place) and then sit in the sun and count your winnings. Admire the grace of movement as up to a dozen impeccably groomed beasts pace twice round the 1000m (⅔ mile) Marsa Race Track; the circuit has been there since 1868. Immediately outside the arena, some of the 700 trotters registered with the Malta Racing Club are stabled. Trotting is Malta's most popular spectator sport and regularly attracts crowds of up to 4000.

## Spectator Sports

*Bocci* (see page 41)
*Federation of Bocci Clubs, ⊠ 55 Sisters Street,Tarxien, ☎ 21696787, ✆ 21696787.*

### Cricket

*Malta Cricket Association, ⊠ Marsa Sports and Country Club, Marsa, ☎ 21233851, ✆ 21242259.*

### Football

International and premier league matches are played at the National Stadium at Ta' Qali. Contact Malta Football Association, *⊠ 280 St Paul Street, Valletta, ☎ 21222697, ✆ 21248489, ✆ grechalv@ euroweb.net.mt ⊕ September–May.*

### Hockey

*Hockey Association of Malta, ⊠ 3 Peprina Court, 3 Nicolo Isouard Street, Sliema, ☎ 21345770, ✆ 21224644.*

### Horse-Racing and Trotting

*Marsa Racing Club, ⊠ Racecourse Street, Marsa, ☎ 21224800, ⊕ Sunday afternoons, Oct–May.*

### Rugby

*Malta Rugby Football Union, ⊠ Office 13, Regent House, Bisazza Street, Sliema, ☎ 21347704/7.*

### Water Polo

*⊠ National Swimming Pool, University Sports Complex, Tal-Qroqq, ⊕ Saturday evenings in summer.*

## Pubs and Clubs

### Axis
✉ St George's Road, Paceville, ☎ 21373830.

### Bamboo Bar
✉ Dragonara Road, Paceville, ☎ 21375331.

### Best in Town
✉ Ball Street, Paceville, ☎ 21377526.

### Caesar's Night Club
✉ Bay Square, Buġibba, ☎ 21571034.

### City of London
✉ 195 Main Street, St. Julians, ☎ 21331706.

### Dine & Duke's
✉ Corinthia Marina Hotel, St George's Bay, ☎ 21381719.

### Empire
✉ 74/77 St George's Road, Paceville, ☎ 21331120.

### Fuego Salsa Bar
✉ St George's Bay, St Julian's, ☎ 21386746.

### The Heritage Pub and Diner
✉ Gandoffli Street, Buġibba, St.Paul's Bay, ☎ 21585677, 🖳 www.heritagepub.com

### La Grotta
✉ Xlendi Road, Xlendi, ☎ 21551149.

### The Ministry of Time
✉ Ball Street, Paceville, ☎ 21382520.

### The New Mirage Music Club
✉ St George's Road, Paceville, ☎ 21373834.

### O'Casey's
✉ St. George's Bay, ☎ 21373900, ☏ 21314726.

### Reflections
✉ Suncrest Hotel, ☎ 21577101, ☏ 21575478.

### Stownes
✉ Pioneer Road, Buġibba, ☎ 21581223.

### Tattingers
✉ Saqqajja Hill, Rabat, ☎ 21451104.

### Waves
✉ Għadira Bay, Mellieħa, ☎ 21523253.

---

### Nightlife
Malta's nightlife is centred around St Julian's and Sliema, both having a multitude of bars and nightclubs; especially St Julians, where nightclubs and restaurants lie next door to each other, for streets on end. There are also several discotheques, which are really popular. Paceville also has a vibrant nightlife with many popular clubs staying open until the early hours.

---

### The Mnarja Races
Rabat plays a big part in the festival of St Peter and St Paul on 29 June – the Mnarja (it derives from the Latin word *illuminaria*, to light up). The bareback horse and donkey races on the steep Saqqajja hill leading into Rabat from Valletta, have been held since the time of the Knights. Winners are handed banners called *palji* from a gallery at the winning post; they are used as altar cloths for the following year. The feast of Mnarja also comes alive in Buskett Gardens, where crowds gather for a day of high revelry.

**Above:** *The limestone Azure Window near Dwejra Point.*

## EXCURSIONS
## Diving Excursions

The Maltese islands are rich in diving opportunities. These are some of the more popular sites:

### The Tugboat Rozi, Malta

Approximately 120m (400ft) from the old jetty, near Marfa Point, lies the tugboat Rozi. The tugboat sunk in 1991 and is now a popular site for beginners and experts alike.

### Blenheim Bomber, Malta

This well preserved wreck of a World War II bomber is situated 800m (870yd) east of Xorb Il-Ghagin, off the southeast coast, at a depth of 42m (140ft).

### Azure Window and Blue Hole, Dwejra Point, Gozo

The Blue hole, a natural rock formation formed by wind and wave erosion, is located in front of the Azure window, at the bottom of Dwejra Point. The diving area contains many exciting arches and cavities.

### Għasri Valley (The Blue Dome / Cathedral Cave), Gozo

Ghasri Valley is situated between Reqqa Point and Forna Point. The cave's entrance is only 5m (17ft) below the surface and leads into an amazing large domed vault.

### Lighthouse Reef, Comino

Southwest of Comino, a lighthouse marks the location of the reef. This spectacular dive offers varied seascapes including a chimney, boulders, swimthroughs and caverns.

## Southern Villages

**Żurrieq** is one of Malta's oldest parishes. The church of St Catherine dates from 1634 and contains fine works by Mattia Preti. Several buildings date from the Knights' era including the Armeria Palace, a former armoury. The medieval Church of the Annunciation was built on the site of the Ħal Millieri settlement.

Nearby **Qrendi** has three churches – the parish church of Santa Maria by Lorenzo Gafa (1685), St Catherine Tat-Torba and St Saviour's. Near the latter is the Knights' late 16th-century Gwarena Tower, Malta's only octagonal defence.

**Luqa**, the site of Malta International Airport, was almost destroyed in World War II. The rebuilt church of St Andrew, originally from 1650, contains a Mattia Preti altarpiece. Nearer the new terminal is **Gudja**, birthplace of the architect Gerolamo Cassar, with the isolated **St Mary Ta' Bir Miftuħ**, dating from 1430 and one of the original 10 parish churches of Malta.

The road east from Gudja passes through **Għaxaq** to **Żejtun**, dominated by Lorenzo Gafa's church of St Catherine, the dome of which can be seen from afar. Much older is the former church of St Gregory, built in 1436 and enlarged by the Knights.

**Żabbar** boasts one of Malta's most unorthodoxly beautiful churches in the Sanctuary of the Virgin of Grace. On a roundabout on the Fgura side of town is the Hompesch Arch dedicated to the last Grand Master, Ferdinand de Hompesch.

**Church of St Catherine**
✉ 138 Triq il-Karmnu, Żurrieq, ☎ 21642010.

**Church of the Annunciation**
✉ Ħal Millieri,
☎ 21642010.

**Church of Santa Maria**
✉ Triq il-Parrocca, Qrendi, ☎ 21649395.

**Church of St Andrew**
✉ 52 Misrah tal-Knisja, Luqa, ☎ 21809310.

**St Mary Ta' Bir Miftuh**
✉ 2 Triq il-Kappillan Gudja, ☎ 21696039.

**Church of St Catherine**
✉ 2 Triq San Girgor, Zejtun, ☎ 21694563.

**Church of St Gregory**
✉ 2 Triq San Girgor, Zejtun, ☎ 21821801.

**Sanctuary of the Virgin of Grace**
✉ 22 Triq is-Santwarju, Żabbar, ☎ 21824383.

**Below:** *Festa time in Żurrieq. Flags adorn the streets by St Catherine's church.*

<u>Red (St Agatha)</u>
<u>Tower</u>
**Location:** Map D–B2
**Distance from**
**Valletta:** approximately.
22km (13.7 miles)
✉ Marfa Ridge
🕘 Although the tower
is not open to the pub-
lic, the surrounding hill-
side has excellent views
and an enjoyable walk.

## Marfa Ridge

The high ground beyond Mellieħa Bay belongs to the Marfa Ridge, protected by the 1649 **Red Tower** of the Knights. Driving along the narrow ridge road past the Red Tower to **Ras il-Qammieħ**, there are stunning views across the Comino Channel to Gozo and Comino.

From a shrine at the crest of the hill, the narrow, pot-holed road on the right follows the ridge to the **Madonna statue** and a tiny **chapel** on a remote and windy part of the island, favoured by the hunting fraternity.

All the side lanes from the ridge road head down across the rugged landscape to little bays beyond the ridge. These include **Ramla Bay**, **Armier Bay** with its blue-and-green-painted holiday homes and the attractive yet oddly named **Slug Bay**, situated below the **White Tower**. These bays attract many more Maltese than tourists, who tend to favour bigger stretches like Mellieħa Bay and Golden Bay. In winter, the extreme north of the island is deserted, its holiday homes barred and bolted – as such, it makes fine walking country.

A few hundred metres before reaching the Gozo ferry terminal at Ċirkewwa, a side road leads uphill to a small cliff-top car park overlooking **Paradise Bay**.

**Below:** *The Knights'*
*Red (St Agatha)*
*Tower fortification.*

80

## Comino

In the middle of the channel between Malta and Gozo sits the island of Comino, all 2.5 km² (1 sq mile) of it, which can be reached from both Malta and Gozo. Historically a pirates'

**Above:** *The Comino Tower, guarding the channel between Malta and Gozo.*

haven, Comino is today the refuge of tourists seeking solitude, relaxation and every water sport under the furnace-like summer sun. There are no cars or roads on Comino; a short coastal path links the island's low-rise four-star tourist accommodation, the Comino Hotel and Comino Bungalows, in adjacent bays.

From the Gozo ferry, you can make out the sparkling turquoise waters of the **Blue Lagoon** on the fractured coast between Comino and the islet of Cominotto. From mid-morning to early afternoon it usually has a full complement of tourist boats and is a favourite haunt of scuba divers, who have plenty to explore in the fascinating underwater world of caves and grottos.

The island's dominant feature is the **Comino Tower**, built in 1618 by Grand Master Alof de Wignacourt to protect the Comino Channel from raiders and later used as a hunting lodge. There are also the remains of a former isolation hospital used by the British in World War I, the small Gothic **St Mary's Chapel**, (dating from the late 1600s in which masses are still held), possibly the world's smallest police station and a pig farm. A handful of people live on the island year-round.

**Blue Lagoon**
Location: Map D–A1
⊠ Between Cominotto and the west end of the island.
🕑 From 10:00–16:00 in summer, Blue Lagoon is crowded.

**Comino (St Mary's) Tower**
Location: Map D–A1
🕑 Not open to the public.

**St Mary's Chapel**
Location: Map D–A1
⊠ Santa Marija Bay.

## Excursions

*Above: Gozo's chief resort, Marsalforn, was once a small fishing village.*

### Xerri's Grotto
Location: Map B–C2
Distance from Victoria: approximately 3km (1.9 miles)
✉ Gnien Imrik Street, Xaghra.
☎ 21560572.
💰 50c.
🕐 Daily: 09:00–18:00.

### Ninu's Cave
Location: Map B–C2
Distance from Victoria: approximately 3km (1.9 miles)
✉ 17 January Street, Xaghra.
☎ 21556863.
💰 25c.
🕐 Daily: 08:30–18:00.

## Gozo

Most visitors to Gozo are day-trippers, arriving by ferry in mid-morning and leaving in late afternoon, but to fully appreciate Gozo you need to stay for a bit longer.

**Victoria**, Gozo's capital, begs comparison with Mdina. The island's main roads radiate from the capital and you need a map to find your way around. Victoria is, however, a place to visit rather than to stay, as there are no hotels and few restaurants.

Crowned by its mighty **Church of Our Lady of Victories**, **Xagħra** (pronounced Shar-ra) dominates Gozo's northern landscape. Nearby is the well-restored **Ta-Kola Windmill** of 1725, one of several that once dotted the island, and now a small museum. Two limestone caves – **Ninu's Cave** and **Xerri's Grotto** – have fascinating stalactites and stalagmites. Further north, **Marsalforn** is Gozo's most popular resort (*see page 33*).

Western Gozo's coastline of cliffs and caves strikes a pleasing contrast with the deep blue Mediterranean. Erosion has created a fine natural arch, the **Azure Window** (*see page 78*). Offshore in Dwejra Bay is **Fungus Rock**, whose unusual vegetation cover was prized by the Knights as a cure for dysentery and haemorrhaging. A third geological feature is the **Inland Sea**, a sheltered seawater pool linked by a natural passageway to the sea.

Of Gozo's smaller villages, **Għarb** is among the prettiest. Its ornate houses cluster around the Church of the Immaculate Conception. Within a kilometre of Għarb are the hamlets of **Birbuba**, **Għammar** and

**Santa Pietru**. At the top of the road leading downwards to **Dwejra Point** is **San Lawrenz**; to the right of the road which heads back towards Victoria is the **Ta' Dbiegi Craft Village** (*see* page 53) . The national shrine of **Ta' Pinu Basilica** is situated between Għarb and Għammar.

The cliffs of southern Gozo are the highest on the island, rising nearly 150m (500ft) either side of Xlendi Bay. **Xlendi** (*see* page 33) sits at the seaward end of a valley; halfway down, a side road heads eastwards to Munxar. Occupying two hills either side of the Hanzira Valley beyond Munxar are the villages of Xewkija and Sannat. The scenic road to Xlendi descends from Victoria with views across to Munxar. It passes the **Knights' Wash House** in Fontana, built over a spring that supplied the locals with water.

**Sannat** is known for its lacemaking and for a really outstanding hotel, Ta' Ċenċ. Between Sannat and Xewkija, a narrow lane leads down through the Hanzira Valley to the attractive inlet of Mġarr ix-Xini, a quiet spot, good for bathing.

**Mġarr** is the main port of entry from Malta. The view from the ferry is of a busy little harbour packed with boats and a skyline pierced by the spires of two churches – Our Lady of Lourdes and the church of Għajnsielem. North of Mġarr is the large and prosperous village of Nadur, where the splendid Parish Church of St Peter and St Paul contains some fine stained glass. Beyond Nadur and Qala there are the small but exquisite beaches of San Blas and Hondoq bays (*see* page 33).

---

**Ta-Kola Windmill**
Location: Map B–C2
Distance from Victoria: approximately 3km (1.9 miles)
✉ Windmill Square, Xagħra. Situated just off Ġgantija temples.
☎ 21560820/ 21561071.
💰 Lm1 (ticket also valid for Ġgantija temples, *see* page 27).
🕐 08:30–16:30 Mon–Sat; 08:30–15:00 Sundays year-round.

**Below:** *Dwejra's cliffs aglow at sunset.*

**Above:** *A blue lamp in evidence at St Paul's Bay police station.*

## Best Times to Visit

Valletta, Mdina, the Three Cities and the resorts are best explored out of the peak holiday months of July and August, when there are fewer tourists and it is not quite so hot. Malta's southern part is best seen in late spring, if only for appreciating the greenery and wild flowers. Take in Rabat in late June, when the Mnarja horse races are held as part of the festival of St Peter and St Paul. Summer is most popular for visiting Malta's north, with the beaches attracting thousands between June and September. Winter vacationers should stay in Sliema or St Julian's, where there is much more going on out of season. The centre of Malta, as well as Gozo and Comino, are best enjoyed in spring, when visitors can view the fine rural aspects and admire the wild flowers.

## Tourist Information

Malta Tourist Offices are in Austria (Vienna), France (Paris), Germany (Frankfurt), Holland (Amsterdam), Italy (Milan), Russia (Moscow), Sweden (Stockholm), the United Kingdom (London) and the USA (New York).

**The Malta Tourism Authority** ✉ *229 Merchants Street, Valletta,* ☎ *22915000* ✆ *info@visitmalta.com* 🖳 *www.visitmalta.com* **Tourist Information Offices** within Malta can be found at: ✉ *Malta International Airport (arrivals lounge),* ☎ *2169996073;* ✉ *1 City Gate, Valletta,* ☎ *21237747;* ✉ *1 Palm Street, Victoria, Gozo,* ☎ *21558106;* and ✉ *Mġarr Harbour, Gozo,* ☎ *21553343.*

## Entry Requirements

Nationals of most countries, including the UK, may enter Malta for up to three months on production

# TRAVEL TIPS

of a valid passport. A visa is required in a few cases. Non-Maltese travellers must complete an embarkation or disembarkation card before passport control, whether on arrival or departure.

## Customs
Duty-free allowances are 200 cigarettes (or 50 cigars, 100 cigarillos or 250g of tobacco), one litre bottle of spirits and one litre bottle of wine, and a reasonable amount of perfume and eau de toilette per adult visitor. Gifts to residents valued at more than Lm50 are subject to customs duty. Duty-free shops are in the arrival and departure halls at Malta International Airport; there are no duty-free shops at the Sea Passenger Terminal, but several other outlets in the area are licensed to sell duty-free goods.

## Health Requirements
No health precautions

are needed by visitors to Malta. Smallpox and cholera vaccination certificates are required by arrivals from infected areas and yellow fever immunization by travellers arriving within six days of leaving an infected area.

## Getting to Malta
**By air:** The national airline, Air Malta, operates direct scheduled services to Malta International Airport from some 45 points throughout Europe, the Middle East and North Africa; from the UK, British Airways also operates. Malta is also served by airlines of many other European countries, including Alitalia, and Lufthansa. It is also possible to book seats on charter flights operating to Malta – contact your travel agent. Flight inquiries within Malta, ☎ 21249600.
To contact **Air Malta** ✉ *Malta International Airport, Gudja*

☎ *2122999884,*
✆ *2122999368,* ☝ *info@airmalta.com.mt*
🖥 *www.airmalta.com*
✉ *Malta International Airport, Luqa,*
☎ *21249600,*
✆ *21249563,* 🖥 *www.maltairport.com*
**By sea:** The high-speed catamaran services of Virtu Ferries, ☎ *21318854,*
✆ *21345221,* 🖥 *www.virtuferries.com* operate from Pozzallo, Catania and Licata in Sicily to Malta. The Gozo Channel Company, ☎ *21556016,* operates the inter-island service which runs between Malta and Gozo.

## What to Pack
In summer the minimum is required – lightweight casual clothing which can be easily washed suffices and you don't need to take pullovers, cardigans or jackets as it stays warm until late evening. If you burn easily, take something to cover the shoulders and arms as Malta's sun

85

can be intense. Children should wear a teeshirt over their swimwear in the pool or sea to prevent burning. Take sunglasses, too – the strong sun reflects off Malta's light-coloured buildings with real intensity. If you feel like glamming up in the evening you won't feel out of place, as the Maltese tend to dress up rather than down when they go out. In winter, although temperatures might look good, warm clothing is necessary as the air can be damper than expected and the stone buildings can be cold.

## Money Matters

**Currency:** There are 100 cents to the lira. Notes are Lm2, Lm5, Lm10 and Lm20; coins are Lm1 and 1, 2, 5, 10, 25 and 50 cents.
**Exchange:** Malta's two main banks are the Bank of Valletta and HSBC; both have branches throughout the island with currency exchange facilities.

There is a 24-hour exchange facility at Malta International Airport. Other banks include Lombard Bank and APS Bank. Smaller bureaux de change are found in Valletta as well as other tourist areas.

The maximum sum in local currency allowed in and out of the country is Lm1000 per person. To change Maltese currency back, it is necessary to present exchange receipts.

Bank **opening hours** show seasonal variation. Summer (15 June–30 Sept): 08:00–14:00 Monday to Thursday, 08:00–15:30 Friday, 08:15–11:30 Saturday; winter (1 Oct–14 June): 08:30–12:45 or 14:00 Monday to Thursday, 08:30–12:45 or 15:30 Friday, 08:30–12:00 or 12:15 Saturday. Some of the branches are open for longer hours than these.

Foreign exchange facilities are also selectively available in summer from 16:00–19:00 and in winter from 15:00–18:00.
**Credit cards:** International credit cards are widely accepted in hotels, restaurants and most shops but expect to have to use cash in the smaller shops, bars and snack-bars.
**Tipping:** Taxi drivers should be tipped 10%; restaurants also 10%, unless a service charge has been added to the bill; porters and tourist guides a minimum of Lm1.
**Taxes:** VAT at 10–15% was reintroduced in Malta from 1998. Prices displayed include VAT; the law states that a receipt must be given and retained by the customer for at least 24 hours.

## Transport

Though substantial investment in Malta's road system in recent years has improved internal communications, journey times are generally slow and the Valletta–Sliema–St Julian's conurbation, Hamrun and Birkirkara can be especially busy. The underground multi-storey car park for 1800 cars outside Valletta's City Gate is handy for the capital, as parking within Valletta is severely restricted by the narrowness of the roads.

While road sign-posting has been improved, you will probably still find yourself navigating by the sun in remoter country areas where signs are occasional or non-existent. In Gozo this is less of a problem – most of the roads radiate from the island's capital, Victoria.

**Road:** Car hire in Malta is among the cheapest in the Mediterranean; rates are fully inclusive and the daily rate usually works out cheaper if the car is hired for a week or longer. Even hiring a car at Malta Airport can pay for three days rental by saving a Lm10 taxi fare each way. International car rental companies such as Avis, Hertz, Budget and Europcar operate alongside local companies, of which Alpine and Wembleys are two of the largest.

All valid national driving licences and international driving licences are recognized. While Maltese law allows driving from 18 years with no upper age limit, some companies restrict car hire to those over 25 and under 70. If you are involved in an accident, call the police; do not move the car before the police have made their on-the-spot report, or it may invalidate your insurance.

**Road rules:** Driving is on the left in Malta, a legacy of British rule. Many Maltese do however prefer the middle of the road (it's the shortest route and avoids the bumps),

---

**Useful Phrases**

*kemm?* • How much?
*kemm boghod?* • How far?
*bonġu* • Good morning
*bonswa* • Good evening
*il-lejl it-tajjeb* • Good night
*saħħa* • Goodbye
*kif int?* • How are you?
*lejn ix-xellug* • To the left
*lejn il-lemin* • To the right
*grazzi* • Thanks
*grazzi ħafna* • Thanks very much
*skużani* • Excuse me
*skużi* • I beg your pardon
*jekk jogħġbok* • Please
*jiddispjaċini* • Sorry
*għal bejgħ* • For sale
*għoli wisq* • Too dear
*irħis ħafna* • Very cheap

## Place Names

Pronunciation difficulties are caused by accented letters (ċ = *ch*; ġ = *j*; ż = *ts*) and silent letters (għ; h, though aspirated at the end of a word; and q). Other pronunciations are: ħ = *h*; j = *y*; x = *sh*; m = *im* when an initial letter and followed by a consonant, as in Mdina. You may find yourself having to pronounce the following:

Dwejra (*d'way-rah*)
Ġgantija (*jee-gann-tee-yah*)
Għar Lapsi (*ahr-lapp-see*)
Għar Dalam (*ahr-dall-am*)
Għarb (*ahrb*)
Għasri (*ahs-ree*)
Ħaġar Qim (*ha-jah-eem*)
Lija (*lee-yah*)
Luqa (*loo-ah*)
Marsaxlokk (*mar-sah-shlok*)
Mdina (*im-deen-ah*)
Mġarr (*im-jarr*)
Mnajdra (*im-na-eed-ra*)
Mqabba (*im-ab-ba*)
Msida (*im-see-dah*)
Naxxar (*nash-shar*)
Qala (*ahl-ah*)
Qawra (*ow-rah*)
Qormi (*orr-me*)
Qrendi (*ren-dee*)
Siġġiewi (*sij-jee-e-wee*)
Ta' Ċenċ (*ta chench*)
Tarxien (*tar-she-en*)
Xagħra (*shuh-ra*)
Xewkija (*show-kee-yah*)
Xlendi (*shlen-dee*)
Żebbuġ (*zeb-booj*)
Żejtun (*zay-toon*)
Żurrieq (*zuhr-ree*)

and the popular 1980s song *Maltese Calypso* made the now famous reference to the Maltese 'driving in the shade'. Local driving habits are unpredictable (to say the least) and call for vigilance, but pottering sedately around the roads of Malta and Gozo in the company of 170,000 other vehicles, beats motorway driving any day. The speed limit is 50kph (30mph) in built-up areas and 80kph (50mph) elsewhere. Road signs are international; traffic lights have been installed throughout the island in the last few years. Petrol stations sell super grade as well as unleaded. They now have self-service operating pumps which remain open until 22:00 everyday.

**Taxis:** Travelling by taxi is not cheap and fares increase sharply after midnight. Taxis are white (usually Mercedes), with the letters TY on the white number plate. They are metered to display government-controlled prices, although the meter is not always switched on – if this is the case, make sure that you agree on the fare in advance. Taxis are readily available at the airport and on ranks in the main resort areas; some of the larger hotels have their own rank. Note that Maltese taxis do not cruise the streets in the hope of picking up a fare. It is possible to hire a taxi for a day's sightseeing, but again agree to the price first. For a 24-hour taxi service in Malta ☎ 21345353, 21332074, 21345454.

**Buses:** A ride on one of Malta's old yellow bone-shaker buses should not be missed. Public transport in Malta operates frequently and is amazingly cheap. Most fares are 15 cents although some direct routes cost more. Routes radiate from the Valletta bus terminus outside City Gate to every town, village and sandy beach in the island. In Gozo, buses (grey with a red stripe) serve the main villages from Victoria but run infrequently.

**Ferry:** A ferry service operates half-hourly in summer from the Strand in Sliema, (the area is still referred to as the Ferries from the steam ferries of old), across Marsamxett Harbour to Valletta. It is a good alternative to the road trip – and quicker, too. Departure times are advertised at the Sliema departure point.

The **Gozo ferry** service is operated by The Gozo Channel Company. The 6km (4-mile) crossing from Ċirkewwa in north-west Malta to Mġarr in Gozo takes about 20 minutes. The car-carrying service operates more or less hourly in summer (every two hours at night); the frequency changes from late September to late June, when there are no night sailings. Winter crossings can be affected by weather conditions – if in doubt, check with the Gozo Channel Company, ☎ 21243964; in Gozo, 21556016. ♿ Return fares are Lm5.75 for a car and driver, Lm1.75 per adult and 50c per child and senior citizen, confusingly paid at a kiosk on the Gozo side before the return journey.

**Helicopter:** The 10-minute helicopter journey between Malta International Airport and Xewkija in Gozo, is the quickest connection between the islands. Primarily intended for passengers arriving and departing through Malta International Airport and connecting to and from Gozo, the service easily allows for a day return trip to either island – there are up to 18 flights daily each way in summer. Advance reservation is recommended, ☎ 2122999138 in Malta; 21557905 or 21561301 in Gozo; or see a travel agent. Malta Air Charter also operates helicopter sightseeing.

## Business hours

**Offices:** Offices in Malta and Gozo switch over to summer working hours for July, August and September – generally 07:30–13:30. For the rest of the year, working hours are 08:30–17:00 with a break for lunch.

**Shops:** Shops are open from 09:00–13:00 and again from 16:00–19:00 Mon–Sat; closed on Sundays and public holidays (see page 50). Many shops in tourist areas stay open throughout the day.

## Time

Malta is on Central European Time, one hour ahead of Greenwich Mean (Universal Standard)

Time in winter and two hours ahead of GMT from the last Sunday in March to the last Sunday in September. The islands are six hours ahead of the USA's Eastern Standard Winter Time and seven hours ahead in summer.

## Communications

Big investment in Malta's telephone system has worked wonders in recent years, for making both local and international calls.

Most of the telephone numbers in Malta and Gozo are eight-figure numbers starting with '21' and there is no area code. To call Malta from abroad, dial the international access code followed by 356. For local inquiries in Malta as well as in Gozo, dial 190, and for international (overseas) inquiries, dial 194.

The Telemalta Corporation provides a 24-hour phone and fax service from its St Julian's office; other phone/ fax offices around the island are located in South Street, Valletta; Bisazza Street, Sliema; Qawra; St Paul's Bay; Malta International Airport (on the ground floor); and Victoria on Gozo.

STD dialling is available to most countries, including the UK (code 0044), USA and Canada (001), South Africa (0027) and Australia (0061). Phone cards valued from Lm2–5 can be purchased from any Telemalta branch, post offices, some banks as well as some newsagents.

There are **post offices** in most towns and villages; they are usually open from 07:45–13:30 but these hours can vary. The main post office in St Zachary Street, Valletta, is open until 18:00 on weekdays; Gozo's main post office is situated in Republic Street, Victoria. Stamps are available from certain newsagents in some of the towns and villages.

## Electricity

The power supply is 240 volts, single phase, 50 cycles. Standard (UK) rectangular three-pin plugs are needed.

## Weights and Measures

Malta uses the metric system for all measurements.

## Health Services

There are two general hospitals in the islands: St Luke's at Gwardamanġa, near Valletta, ☎ 21241251; and Gozo General hospital in Gozo, ☎ 21561600.

There are health clinics in several towns and villages.

Pharmacies are open Mon–Sat from 08:30–13:00 and 15:00–19:00; on Sunday, one pharmacy per district opens in the morning on a roster listed in the newspapers (or call Police HQ, ☎ 21224001).

Most hotels have the services of a doctor on call. In an emergency, ☎ 196 in Malta or 21556851 in Gozo. Malta has reciprocal health agreements with the UK and Australia.

## Health Precautions

Visitors to Malta do not need to have any innoculations, but should take care with sunbathing – remember that Malta is further south than parts of North Africa and that the sun deserves more respect than usual.

## Emergencies

On Malta, dial police ☎ 191 (general inquiries, ☎ 224992), ambulance ☎ 196 and fire ☎ 199. On Gozo, dial police ☎ 562044, ambulance ☎ 196 and fire ☎ 562040. There are police stations in most of the villages.

## Etiquette

As Malta is a strongly religious country, visitors to the cathedrals and churches should dress accordingly to save causing offence. Men should ideally wear long trousers rather than shorts (although this is rarely, if ever, enforced); women should cover their shoulders (a wrap may be available at the church door) and avoid wearing shorts or mini-skirts. Topless sunbathing is against the law.

## Language

While Malti is the national language, English is widely spoken and understood, particularly in the resorts.

## Useful Websites

www.visitmalta.com
www.aboutmalta.com
www.travel2malta.com
www.budgettravel.com/malta.htm
www.imalta.com
www.gozo.gov.mt
www.holidays-malta.com

---

<u>Counting</u>
**wiehed** • one
**tnejn** • two
**tlieta** • three
**erbgha** • four
**hamsa** • five
**sitta** • six
**sebgha** • seven
**tminja** • eight
**disgha** • nine
**ghaxra** • ten
**hdax** • eleven
**tnax** • twelve
**ghoxrin** • twenty
**mija** • one hundred

---

<u>Further Reading</u>
**Attard, Joseph**. *Britain and Malta – The Story of an Era*. Publishers Enterprises Group, Malta.
**Blouet, Brian**. *The Story of Malta*. Progress Press, Malta.
**Bradford, Ernle**. *The Great Siege – Malta 1565*. Penguin Books, London.
**Bradford, Ernle**. *Siege of Malta 1940/1943*. Penguin Books, London.
**Gerada, Eric & Zuber, Chris**. *Malta – An Island Republic*. Editions Delroisse.
**Monsarrat, Nicholas**. *The Kappillan of Malta*. Pan, London.
**Ross, Geoffrey Aquilina**. *Images of Malta*. Miranda Publications, Malta.

# INDEX OF SIGHTS

# GENERAL INDEX

# GENERAL INDEX

# GENERAL INDEX